TURKEY

• THE BIRD FOR ALL SEASONS •

By Kristie Alm and Pat Sayre

Illustrated by Jamie Buckiewicz

TURKEY
THE BIRD FOR ALL SEASONS

Published by: Good Time Press
                15707 North East 153rd
                Woodinville, Washington 98072

Copyright © 1984 by Kristie Alm and Pat Sayre

Printed by Dynagraphics, Inc., Portland, Oregon

Layout and Design, Dan Hayes

Library of Congress Catalog Card Number: 84 – 80637
ISBN 0 – 9613344 – 0 – 1

Second Printing, August 1985

Dedication

We dedicate this book to our families and friends in Oregon and Washington who have tasted and tested our turkey recipes. We thank you for your patience and your suggestions, but above all, your discriminating taste!!

Introduction

TURKEY, THE BIRD FOR ALL SEASONS, is a cookbook with a new approach to a traditional old favorite. It will take you beyond the concept of turkey just for the holidays and teach you to take advantage of turkey's economy, versatility, and low-fat-high-protein content. It will encourage you to enjoy turkey in nutritious and delicious meals throughout the year.

It is entirely possible to feed a family of six for an entire week with one twenty (20) pound bird. The cost is minimal and each meal can be distinctive and exciting. We know. We have tried it! Turkey can be used in place of pork, veal, or chicken. It can be stir-fried, pot-roasted, marinated, simmered, sauteed, baked, grilled or curried. The possibilities are endless and the results amazing.

Presented in a clear, understandable format with generous servings, these recipes range from tasty appetizers to a traditional turkey feast with all the trimmings. The soups, which originate from low-fat, low-salt turkey stock, are both hearty and delicate. The sandwiches as well as the salads are a combination of old standbys and innovative new ideas with lots of room for variations. The international main dishes transform the "left-over" turkey into quick, easy, and appetizing family dinners as well as elaborate crowd pleasers. The cutlets are a relatively new concept which will surprise and delight you. They can be prepared as an elegant gourmet entree smothered in rich sauce, or simply braised with herbs and spices.

Although there are many turkey products on the market, our primary objective in this cookbook is the bird itself. The explicit diagrams will teach you to carve the uncooked turkey into sections and cook the sections separately. This is by far the best bargain and the most practical use of the turkey.

Artfully illustrated with humorous turkey characters, this cookbook is the perfect gift, entertaining as well as instructive. Whether you are a beginning cook who needs clear, defined direction, or a gourmet who likes room to experiment, this book will inspire you all year long.

TURKEY IS, INDEED, THE BIRD FOR ALL SEASONS.

TABLE OF CONTENTS

How to Thaw a Turkey

There are several methods for thawing a turkey. We will give them all to you as different methods work differently depending on how much time is available. They are all perfectly safe and acceptable.

1. Refrigerator Method: This is the safest method and is most highly recommended. It also takes the longest time. Leave the turkey in the original wrap and put it in the refrigerator for several days, depending on the size of the bird. Allow 1 day (24 hours) defrosting time for each 5 pounds of turkey.

2. Cold Running Water Method: Leave the turkey in its original wrap and put it in the sink. Run cold water slowly over the bird. Let it continue to run but be sure to turn the turkey often (about once every half hour). Allow about 30 minutes defrosting time for each pound of turkey.

3. Submerged in Cold Water Method: Leave the turkey in its original wrap and put it in a deep sink completely submerged in cold water. It is necessary to change the water about every 30 minutes as the water gets too cold to do much good. Allow about 30 minutes defrosting time for each pound of turkey.

Thawing a turkey at room temperature, especially a large bird, is not recommended because parts of the bird thaw fast and become too warm. This can encourage the growth of bacteria.

A thawed turkey works perfectly when you have time to thaw it and want to cook the whole bird. However, our favorite way to use a turkey is either to buy it fresh, carve it into sections (see page 7), and freeze those sections not needed immediately, or to ask your butcher to cut a frozen bird into quarters (completely in half and then the hindquarters from the breast), and then refreeze and use as needed. This is by far the best bargain and the most economical and versatile use of the turkey.

How to Carve an Uncooked Turkey

For best results, start with a carving board, and a very sharp knife. Place the thawed (or fresh) bird breast-side up on the carving board before you, with the legs on your right. Reverse if you're left-handed.

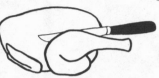

1. **Grasp the drumstick. Slit the skin between the thigh and the body and cut through the joint. Remove the entire hindquarter by pulling it away from the body until the ball and socket hip joint is exposed. Use the point of the knife to disjoint the socket. Sever the wing by using the same method as with the hindquarter. Repeat on the other side.**

2. **Turn the breast so the breast bone faces you. Cut out the entire breast section by placing the tip of the knife along one side of the breast bone and begin cutting through the skin as close to the bone as possible, pulling the meat away as you cut.**

3. **Continue cutting and pulling along the breast bone and the ribs until the breast section falls free. Repeat on the other side.**

4. **Cut off any remaining meat and reserve it for recipes calling for pieces of uncooked turkey. Reserve all the bones and the back pieces for stock (see page 19).**

Appetizers

Tahitian Roll-Ups

Makes 24 appetizers

4 large uncooked turkey cutlets
2 cups turkey stock
4 teaspoons curry powder
24 small lettuce leaves (Bibb or green leaf)
Tahitian Sauce (see below)
1 cup toasted coconut (325 degrees for 10 minutes)

1. In sauce pan, combine cutlets, stock and curry powder. Bring to a boil, reduce heat and simmer about 15 minutes. Refrigerate in stock until cool.

2. Remove turkey and cut each cutlet into 6 lengthwise strips.

3. Place each strip of turkey on each lettuce leaf. Fold end of lettuce and roll up. Secure with wooden toothpick. Refrigerate at least 1 hour.

4. Prepare sauce and spoon into small bowl.

5. Spoon coconut into another small bowl.

6. On a tray or platter, arrange lettuce-wrapped turkey around the bowls of sauce and coconut.

7. To serve, dip turkey rolls into sauce and then roll in coconut.

Tahitian Sauce

Combine together:

    1 cup sour cream
    2 tablespoons finely chopped peanuts
    1/4 cup finely chopped chutney

Curried Appetizer Puffs

Puff Dough:

    1/4 cup butter
    1/2 cup water
    1/2 cup flour
    1/8 teaspoon salt
    2 eggs

1. In medium sauce pan, heat butter and water to a rolling boil. Add flour and salt all at once. Stir vigorously over low heat about 1 minute, until mixture becomes smooth and leaves sides of pan.

2. Remove from heat. Beat in 1 egg at a time until mixture loses its gloss.

3. On a lightly greased baking sheet, drop dough by mounded teaspoons. Chill 20 minutes.

4. Bake at 400 degrees for 15 minutes until puffed and golden brown. Cool away from drafts.

Curried Turkey Filling

    2 cups cooked turkey pieces,
      finely chopped
    1/4 cup finely chopped celery
    1 small apple, peeled, cored and
      coarsely grated
    1 tablespoon chopped chives
    1/3 cup mayonnaise
    2 teaspoons curry powder
    1/4 teaspoon salt
    1/4 cup finely chopped peanuts

1. Combine all ingredients and mix well.

2. Cut off top of appetizer puff and spoon in filling. Cover with top. These can be served at room temperature or serve warm by heating in a 350 degree oven for 15 minutes before serving. Do not heat in the microwave.

Hot Hors d'Oeuvre Tarts

Makes 24 tarts

Crust:
1 package (3-ounce) cream cheese
1/2 cup butter, softened
1 cup flour

1. Blend cream cheese and butter. Add flour and mix well.

2. Chill dough at least 1 hour. Divide into 2 dozen 1-inch balls.

3. Place balls in tart cups. Press into sides and bottoms of cups. Cover and chill while you make filling.

Turkey filling:
2 cups cooked turkey pieces, finely chopped
2 teaspoons Dijon mustard
3/4 cup dry bread crumbs, finely crushed
1/4 cup chopped parsley
mayonnaise to blend

1. Combine and fill chilled dough tart cups.

2. Bake 350 degrees for 20 minutes.

Calcutta Turkey Spread

Makes 2 cups

1 cup cooked turkey pieces, finely chopped
1/2 cup mayonnaise
1 tablespoon crystallized ginger, minced (this is found in gourmet section)
2 teaspoons soy sauce
1 teaspoon curry powder
1 tablespoon minced green onion
1 can (8½-ounce) water chestnuts, drained and chopped
sesamé crackers

1. Combine all ingredients, except crackers, into a medium bowl. Mix well.

2. Serve on sesamé crackers.

Dijon-Parmesan Tidbits

Serves 10

**3 cups uncooked turkey pieces cut
    into 1-inch cubes (white meat
    is best)
1/4 cup butter
1 tablespoon Dijon mustard
1 garlic clove, crushed
1 tablespoon minced parsley
1 teaspoon lemon juice
salt to taste
1/4 cup grated Parmesan cheese**

1. Melt butter in a medium skillet. Stir in mustard, garlic, parsley, lemon juice and salt.

2. Add turkey and sauté, turning until turkey is well coated and lightly browned on all sides. Do not overcook.

3. Sprinkle with cheese, tossing until turkey is coated.

4. Serve warm with toothpicks.

Apricot Turkey Treats

Serves 12

**2 cups uncooked turkey chunks
    (white meat is best)
1/4 cup vegetable oil
1/4 cup apricot jam (or apricot-
    pineapple jam)
1/2 cup ketchup
1 green onion, finely chopped
1 teaspoon Worcestershire sauce
1/4 teaspoon salt
3 to 4 drops Tabasco® sauce
toothpicks**

1. In small bowl, combine oil, jam, ketchup, onion, Worcestershire sauce, salt and Tabasco®.

2. Pour over turkey chunks. Cover and refrigerate at least 6 hours or overnight.

3. Drain turkey, reserving liquid. Broil turkey chunks, brushing often with sauce. Turn and broil other side. Do not overcook.

Serve on tray with toothpick in each chunk.

Spicy Turkey Kebabs

Serves 12

**4 cups uncooked turkey breast, cut into
    1-inch chunks
2 tablespoons vegetable oil
1 clove garlic, crushed
1 tomato, peeled, seeded and chopped
1/4 cup peanut butter
1 cup turkey stock
1/2 teaspoon salt
1/4 teaspoon red cayenne pepper
12 to 16 4-inch bamboo skewers**

1. In a sauce pan, heat oil and sauté garlic.

2. Stir in tomato, peanut butter, stock, salt and pepper.

3. Simmer 10 minutes, stirring occasionally. Set aside to cool.

4. Thread 3 or 4 turkey chunks on each skewer and arrange in shallow dish.

5. Pour marinade over turkey, cover and refrigerate 6 or more hours.

6. Broil turkey 3 to 4 inches from heat until browned.

7. Brush with marinade, turn and broil other side. Serve hot.

This can also be done without skewers. Just marinate the turkey chunks, broil as directed and serve each chunk on a toothpick.

Turkey Butter Meatballs

Serves 10

**2 cups ground turkey
1/4 cup melted butter
1/4 teaspoon paprika
1/4 cup mayonnaise
1 tablespoon dried minced onion
    (or fresh onion, minced)
1 egg, beaten
1/2 cup bread crumbs
1/4 cup minced celery
1/2 teaspoon salt
1/8 teaspoon pepper**

1. In a small bowl, combine butter and paprika. Set aside.

2. In a medium bowl, beat egg and add turkey, mayonnaise, onion, bread crumbs, celery, salt and pepper. Mix well (use your hands to mix . . . it works).

3. Shape into 1-inch balls and roll in butter mixture. Arrange in shallow baking dish. (Can be covered and refrigerated or frozen until ready to serve.)

4. Bake at 400 degrees for 15 minutes or until browned and firm. Serve hot with toothpicks.

Cranberry - Barbeque

Serves 16

**3 cups cooked turkey pieces, cut in
    1-inch cubes (white meat is best)**
1 can (8-ounce) jellied cranberry sauce
1/2 cup barbeque sauce
1/8 teaspoon ground allspice
1/2 teaspoon grated orange peel

1. Heat cranberry sauce, barbeque sauce, allspice and orange peel in sauce pan. Simmer about 10 minutes.

2. Pour into chafing dish. Add turkey and heat.

3. Serve warm with toothpicks.

Turkey Pâté

Makes 1¼ cups

1 cup cooked turkey pieces
2 tablespoons butter
1/2 cup chopped almonds
1 tablespoon chopped parsley
1/8 teaspoon salt
1/8 teaspoon pepper
2 tablespoons vegetable oil
3 tablespoons dry white wine
2 tablespoons heavy cream

1. In a small skillet, melt butter and sauté almonds until golden. Drain on paper towel.

2. Place all ingredients in blender or food processor and blend until almost smooth.

3. Serve on crackers.

Soups

Soup

Soup is a very delicious, inexpensive, and nutritious main course when using turkey stock and a combination of vegetables and meat. There is an unlimited variety of ingredients that can be used. This is the time to be creative. Use your imagination.

There are several advantages to making your own soup. It is an inexpensive and relatively simple way to serve a nutritious and complete meal in one dish. Many soups are tastier if made ahead to let the flavors blend. It also can be fat-free since all fat is removed from the turkey stock before it is used. It is an excellent way to control the amount of salt in your diet as you can create rich flavor from the meat, vegetables, herbs and spices with very little salt. In most of our soup recipes we have left the amount of the salt and pepper up to you because so much depends on the strength of the stock and your own personal taste. And don't forget, making soup is a wonderful way to use up leftovers.

Some of our soups call for cream. You can always substitute milk, powdered milk, or low-fat evaporated milk. However, consider that the amount of cream to the total amount of liquid is small, and the difference in flavor is enormous. If you have any creamed soup left over, save it and use it in a recipe calling for canned soup.

Stop!

Turkey Stock

The most important ingredient in soup is the stock, which is the liquid resulting from simmering together meat bones with vegetables, seasonings and water. Stocks are extremely simple to make and can simmer quietly by themselves with little or no attention.

Stock can be refrigerated for at least a week and frozen indefinitely. When freezing, use large containers for soups, and some one-cup containers for sauces. Stock adds flavor and nutrition to the simplest of dishes and we often use it in place of water when cooking vegetables or rice.

The following recipe is a basic stock but don't be limited by it. One person we know used a left-over green salad along with vegetables and the resulting stock was delicious. A word of caution, though, any vegetable with a strong flavor such as broccoli, cauliflower or cabbage could be overpowering.

carcass from turkey (including skin,
    leftover dressing, pan drippings, etc.)
2 carrots, cut in pieces
2 sprigs parsley
2 onions, quartered
3 celery tops
3 teaspoons salt
10 black peppercorns
    (1 teaspoon pepper)
1 bayleaf
1/4 teaspoon thyme
garlic cloves (optional)

1. Break up carcass and place in the largest kettle you've got (or crock pot).

2. Add remaining ingredients and cover with water.

3. Bring to a boil, reduce heat and simmer, covered, for at least 4 hours or overnight. The longer it simmers, the better the flavor.

4. Strain stock through a cheese cloth or a colander into a large bowl.

5. Refrigerate, covered, until fat hardens on top. Skim off fat.

6. Taste the defatted stock. If flavor is weak, boil it down to evaporate some of the water content.

You will need a lighter-flavored stock for creamed soups and sauces and a richer-flavored stock for heartier soups. 19

Basic Cream of . . . Soup

Creamed soups are basically all the same. Use your imagination. Almost any vegetable or combination of vegetables can be used such as celery, asparagus, spinach, broccoli, cauliflower, brussels sprouts, etc. Small bits of turkey or turkey ham added just before serving makes a heartier soup.

**6 cups turkey stock
1 pound fresh vegetable (2 packages
    (10-ounces each) frozen)
chopped onion to taste
3 tablespoons butter
3 tablespoons flour
salt and pepper to taste
2 egg yolks, beaten
1/2 cup cream
    (or milk or evaporated milk)**

1. Sauté the vegetable of your choice (chopped), along with some onion, in 3 tablespoons butter.

2. Add 3 tablespoons flour and cook and stir for 2 minutes.

3. Slowly stir in turkey stock and salt and pepper and simmer until vegetable is tender (the amount of time depends on the vegetable).

4. Puree in a blender or food processor, a little bit at a time, until all soup has been blended. Return to the pan.

5. Combine egg yolks and cream. Add a little of the hot soup to the eggs and cream to heat them, and then stir back briskly into the hot soup.

6. Cook until heated through but do not boil. Add any meat or garnish you desire and serve.

Basic Cream of ... Soup, continued

Variations

1. MUSHROOM: Add juice of 1 lemon to the chopped mushrooms before sautéing.

2. ASPARAGUS: Cut off tips and simmer separately to use as garnish, using remainder of asparagus stalks for the basis of the soup.

3 CAULIFLOWER: Sauté celery along with the onion and cauliflower and garnish with nutmeg or grated cheese.

4. SPINACH: Paprika and/or nutmeg add a good flavoring. Garnish with grated Parmesan cheese. The same thing applies to broccoli.

5. POTATO: Add extra onion or leeks as you sauté the potato. Watercress, parsley, or chives make a nice garnish. If you serve this soup cold, then you have Vichyssoise.

6. CELERY: Garnish with dill (fresh or dried).

7. ONION: Add paprika, nutmeg or Worcestershire sauce.

8. TOMATO: Peel and seed the tomatoes. Add celery to the onion and a little white or brown sugar. Season with parsley or basil and garnish with chives.

Be Adventurous!

Joan's Corn Chowder

Serves 10

3 cups cooked turkey pieces
3 cups turkey stock
4 medium onions, chopped
1/4 cup butter
5 medium potatoes, peeled and diced
2 stalks celery, diced
4 teaspoons salt
1/2 teaspoon pepper
4 cups milk
1 cup light cream
2 cans (17-ounce each) kernel corn
1 can (17-ounce) cream corn
1/4 teaspoon thyme
1½ teaspoon paprika

1. Sauté onions in butter in large kettle until golden brown.
2. Add potatoes, celery, salt, pepper, and turkey stock. Cover and cook for 15 to 20 minutes.
3. Add remaining ingredients and heat slowly. Do not boil.
4. Correct seasonings and serve.

Turkey Lentil Soup

Serves 6

2 cups cooked turkey pieces
6 cups turkey stock (1½ quarts)
2 cans (16-ounce each) stewed tomatoes, cut into pieces
1 large onion, chopped
1½ cup lentils
2 or 3 whole garlic cloves
salt and pepper to taste
3 carrots, diced
1/4 pound fresh spinach, finely chopped
3 stalks celery, chopped
sour cream or yogurt as garnish

1. Add tomatoes, onion, lentils, garlic and seasonings to boiling stock.
2. Cover, reduce heat to simmer, and cook slowly for 2 hours.
3. Add vegetables, bring to a boil, reduce to simmer and cook an additional 1 hour. (Be sure lentils are soft.)
4. Remove garlic cloves.
5. Add turkey and heat thoroughly.
6. Serve with a dollop of sour cream or plain yogurt.

Be still my heart!

Cream of Turkey Soup

Serves 4

2 cups cooked turkey pieces
4 cups rich-flavored turkey stock
1/2 cup chopped celery
1 cup cooked rice
1/2 cup cream
1 tablespoon chopped parsley
salt, pepper and paprika to taste

1. Simmer celery in stock until celery is tender.

2. Add rice and turkey and cook about 5 minutes.

3. Stir a little hot soup into the cream to heat and then add cream to soup.

4. Add parsley and season to taste.

Remember, if you have any creamed soup left over, save it and use it in a recipe calling for canned soup.

Split Pea Soup

Serves 6

6 cups turkey stock
2 cups split peas, washed
2 medium onions, chopped
1 cup chopped celery (leaves included)
2 cloves garlic, pressed
dash of cayenne or Tabasco®
salt and pepper to taste
1 cup grated carrots

1. Place stock and split peas in large kettle.

2. Add onion, celery, garlic and seasonings and cook, covered, on low heat for at least three hours until peas are soft. Stir often to prevent scorching.

3. Before serving, add carrots and simmer until carrots are tender.

Janie's Minestrone

This is a soup for experimenting. There are many variations to try and just about anything works, so be creative, clean out your cupboards and make a soup of your own. Serve with hot biscuits and fruit.

3 cups cooked turkey pieces
1½ quarts (6 cups) turkey stock
1 cup chopped onion
3 tablespoons butter
1 cup diced potato
1 cup sliced carrots
1/2 cup sliced celery
1 cup shredded cabbage
1 can (28-ounce) tomatoes, sliced or
** chunked or stewed**

1/4 cup uncooked rice
1 bay leaf
1/2 teaspoon thyme
1/4 teaspoon basil
salt to taste
1/8 teaspoon pepper
grated Parmesan cheese as garnish

1. Sauté onions in butter until golden brown.
2. Add remaining ingredients, except turkey and cheese.
3. Simmer until vegetables are tender. Remove the bay leaf.
4. Add turkey, heat thoroughly, and garnish with Parmesan cheese.

Variations

1. Substitute 1 cup spinach noodles or your favorite pasta for the rice.
2. Add green beans, peas, corn, zucchini, or any favorite vegetable.
3. Add 1 cup navy beans (soaked overnight).

Greek Lemon Cold Soup

Serves 6

This soup is absolutely refreshing and delicious on a hot, summer day.

6 cups light turkey stock (1½ quarts)
1/4 cup long grain uncooked rice
3 eggs
1/4 cup lemon juice (must be fresh)
salt to taste
1 lemon, thinly sliced

1. In large sauce pan combine stock and rice. Bring to boil, reduce heat, cover and simmer until rice is done (about 20 minutes). Remove from heat.

2. In bowl, beat eggs until fluffy and pale yellow. Beat in lemon juice.

3. Slowly stir 2 cups of hot stock into egg mixture and whisk. Return egg mixture to stock, whisking vigorously until slightly thickened. Season to taste.

4. Cool to room temperature, then refrigerate until icy cold. (The soup will settle slightly. Be sure to stir it before serving.)

5. Garnish with lemon slices.

Turkey Senegalese Soup

Serves 4

1½ cups cooked turkey breast,
**   finely chopped**
3 cups turkey stock
2 tablespoons butter
1½ to 2 teaspoons curry powder
1½ teaspoons flour
1 teaspoon paprika
2 egg yolks, beaten
1/2 cup cream
3 to 4 tablespoons chutney (optional)
salt to taste
chopped chives as garnish

1. In large sauce pan, melt butter, add curry and blend in flour.

2. Slowly stir in stock until smooth and boiling. Add paprika and reduce heat.

3. Combine egg yolks and cream. Add some of the hot soup to heat and then stir slowly into soup until thickened slightly. Do not boil.

4. Add turkey, chutney (if desired) and garnish with chives.

French Onion Soup

The trick to a good onion soup is a long, slow cooking of the onions in butter and oil and then a long, slow simmering in stock in order to achieve a deep, rich flavor.

2 quarts richer-flavored turkey stock
3 tablespoons butter
1 tablespoon oil
1½ pounds yellow onions, thinly
   sliced (about 5 cups)
1 teaspoon salt
1/4 teaspoon sugar
3 tablespoons flour

1/2 cup dry white wine
   (or dry white vermouth)
salt and pepper to taste
3 tablespoons cognac
12 rounds of hard, toasted French bread
   (cut 3/4- to 1-inch thick)
freshly grated Parmesan cheese
   as garnish

1. Prepare bread rounds by baking in 325 degree oven oven 30 minutes until bread is dried out and lightly browned. Sprinkle with olive oil and rub with a garlic clove.
2. Melt butter and oil in large sauce pan. Add onions; cook slowly, covered, 15 minutes over low heat.
3. Uncover, raise heat to medium and stir in salt and sugar (sugar helps to brown the onions). Cook for 30 to 40 minutes, stirring frequently, until onions have turned a deep golden brown.
4. Add flour and stir until blended thoroughly.
5. Combine stock and wine and add to onions. Simmer, partially covered, for 30 to 40 minutes. Season to taste.
6. Just before serving, add cognac.
7. Place rounds of bread in bottom of soup tureen or individual soup bowls and ladle soup over. Sprinkle with Parmesan cheese.

Variation

1. Prepare soup as directed in preceding recipe, omitting step #6.
2. Pour soup into tureen.
3. Stir in 1/2 cup grated Swiss cheese and 1 tablespoon grated raw onion.
4. Float bread rounds in soup and cover with 1½ cups grated Swiss cheese and sprinkle with 1 tablespoon olive oil.
5. Bake at 325 degrees for 20 minutes, then broil for 2 minutes or until cheese is lightly browned. Serve at once.

Leek or Onion Soup

2 quarts turkey stock
3 to 4 peeled potatoes, sliced or diced
3 cups sliced leeks, include tender green parts (yellow onions can be substituted)
1 teaspoon salt
4 to 6 tablespoons heavy cream
2 to 3 tablespoons softened butter
2 to 3 tablespoons minced parsley or chives

1. Simmer potatoes, leeks, stock and salt together partially covered for 40 to 50 minutes.

2. Mash vegetables in the soup with a potato masher, or place through a food mill (do not puree).

3. Just before serving, turn off heat and add cream and butter.

4. Pour into soup tureen and garnish with parsley or chives.

Variations

1. Add to the potatoes and leeks any vegetable you like such as string beans, cauliflower, broccoli, peas, etc.

2. WATERCRESS SOUP: Follow original recipe adding 1 cup chopped watercress leaves. Substitute parsley or chives with small handful of watercress which has boiled 30 seconds in water, then rinsed in cold water, and drained.

3. VICHYSSOISE: Follow original recipe except puree instead of mashing for a smoother soup. Turn off heat. Stir in 1/2 to 1 cup heavy cream. Season to taste (you need more salt in a cold soup). Chill and garnish with chives.

Orange Carrot Soup

This soup is delicious served hot or cold.

6 cups turkey stock
1 tablespoon butter
1 pound carrots, peeled and cut into 2-inch chunks
3 medium onions, coarsely chopped
2 garlic cloves, chopped
1/3 cup flour
1 teaspoon sugar
juice of one orange (about 1/4 cup)
1 cup heavy cream
salt and pepper to taste
1 cup chopped watercress for garnish

1. In a large sauce pan, melt butter, add carrots, onions and garlic. Sauté for about 5 minutes.

2. Blend in flour and gradually add stock. Bring to a boil, cover and simmer 20 minutes. Add sugar and simmer an additional 10 minutes.

3. Puree soup in processor or blender, a little at a time, until all has been blended. Return to pan.

4. Add orange juice and cream and season to taste. Heat thoroughly but do not boil.

5. Garnish with watercress.

If served cold, be sure soup is icy cold for best flavor.

Be adventurous!

Beer Cheese Soup

5 cups turkey stock
1/2 cup butter
1/2 cup finely chopped carrots
1/2 cup finely chopped celery
1/2 cup finely chopped onion
1/2 cup flour
salt to taste
1/2 teaspoon dry mustard
1 tablespoon grated Parmesan cheese
1 cup grated sharp Cheddar cheese
1 can (12-ounce) flat beer (open and
   let sit for a couple of hours)

1. In a large sauce pan, melt butter and sauté carrots, celery and onion until limp.

2. Gradually blend in flour, and add salt and dry mustard. Cook over medium heat until mixture barely begins to brown.

3. Add stock, turning heat to high.

4. Add cheeses and beer, stirring constantly.

5. Bring to boil for only a moment. Reduce heat and serve.

Joanne's Bean Soup

This soup should be made at least one day before serving.

1 cup chopped turkey ham
2 quarts turkey stock
4 cups pinto beans
1 large can (15·ounce) tomato sauce
2 cups chopped onions
2 cloves garlic, chopped
1 can (4·ounces) diced green chiles
2 tablespoons chili powder
salt to taste

1. Bring stock and pinto beans to a boil and let sit one hour.

2. Add rest of ingredients and simmer at least 10 hours.

3. Add stock or water as liquid evaporates. Be sure to stir often so beans won't stick to bottom of pan. (Beans must be very soft and almost unrecognizable.)

4. Add salt just before serving.

5. Serve with warm tortillas.

Try cooking this soup in a crock pot.

You can even cook it all night on low heat.

Aye yi-yi-yi!

Turkey Vegetable-Noodle

2 cups cooked turkey pieces
3 quarts turkey stock
2 cups diced carrots
2 cups diced potatoes
2 cups diced onions
1 teaspoon salt
2 cups chopped green beans
**   (1 package frozen)**
1 cup broken flat egg noodles

1. Bring stock, carrots, potatoes, and onions to a boil and turn off the heat.

2. Add salt and set aside. (This can be done early in the morning.)

3. Twenty minutes before serving, add green beans and noodles.

4. Boil slowly until vegetables and noodles are done.

5. Add turkey meat and simmer. Correct seasonings and serve.

Variations

1. To the preceding recipe add: 1 can (15¼ ounce) kidney beans, drained
                                 1 cup broken spaghetti (in place of noodles)
                                 1/8 teaspoon pepper

2. Substitute 1½ cup cooked barley for the noodles.

3. Add 1 can lima beans and 1 cup chopped celery to the original recipe.

4. Mix together in small bowl: 1 tablespoon tomato paste
                                1/4 cup fresh basil (1½ teaspoons dried)
                                1/2 cup grated Parmesan cheese

   Beat in a drop at a time: 1/4 cup olive

   Just before serving, add 1 cup soup to the tomato mixture and then add mixture to the soup.

   Serve with French bread.

Basic Bisque with Turkey Stock

Serves 8

1 quart turkey stock
1/4 cup butter
1 large onion, chopped
1 cup chopped celery (tops included)
4 cups peeled and cubed potatoes
1/4 cup finely chopped parsley

1/2 teaspoon salt
1/4 teaspoon pepper
1 quart milk
3 tablespoons cornstarch
1/4 cup water
butter
finely chopped parsley

1. In a large kettle, melt butter and sauté onion and celery until limp.
2. Add potatoes, parsley, salt, pepper, and turkey stock.
3. Simmer until potatoes are tender (about 30 minutes).
4. Stir in milk and heat thoroughly. Do not boil.
5. Blend cornstarch with water until smooth. Add slowly to soup, stirring constantly.
6. Continue cooking until soup begins to boil and thicken.
7. Float a generous pat of butter on top and sprinkle with parsley.

Variations

1. SHRIMP BISQUE: Prepare the basic recipe and add 1¼ pounds small, cooked shrimp, or 2 packages (12-ounces each) frozen shrimp, partially thawed, just before adding the cornstarch mixture.

2. CRAB: Prepare basic recipe and add 1 whole bay leaf along with the salt and pepper. Stir in 1 pound crab meat just before adding the cornstarch mixture.

3. MINCED CLAM: Omit the butter from the basic recipe. Cut 5 slices bacon into 1-inch pieces and fry in kettle until bacon is limp. Add the onion and celery to bacon drippings and continue cooking as directed. Stir in 3 cans (10-ounces each) minced clams and the liquid just before adding milk. Heat thoroughly and continue as directed.

4. FISHERMAN'S CHOWDER: Follow directions for MINCED CLAM except use only 1 can clams and add 1 pound firm, white fish (ling cod, halibut, rockfish, bass) cut into 1-inch cubes, and 1 can (17-ounce) whole kernel corn and its liquid. Stir in the milk and continue cooking as directed.

Soup of the Month

Soup is a wonderful way to use up leftovers. All you need is a good, rich, stock and a freezer container in which to store leftovers. During the month, save all leftover meats and drippings (fat removed), vegetables, gravies, pastas, rice . . . you name it . . . and store in the freezer container, adding additional leftovers as the month progresses. When you're ready to make soup, combine the turkey stock with the leftovers, add a little tomato paste, or wine, or soy sauce, or herbs and seasonings, or whatever else sounds good, and you have a great soup. If you need to thicken it, combine flour and water in equal amounts, add some hot soup to that mixture to heat, and then stir back briskly into the soup until it thickens. Combined with a hearty bread and piece of fruit, you've got a nutritious and delicious meal.

We have a friend who "saves" all year long in several freezer containers and once a year combines it all for a magnificent soup for her husband's annual stag poker party. It's an easy and inexpensive way to feed a crowd and they love it.

Another idea is to have a "Make Your Own Soup" meal. Prepare a good, rich, stock and offer bowls of meats and vegetables (fresh or cooked) and let each person create his own, individual soup. Serve it buffet style. This involves little effort and is a good way to feed a crowd and clean out the refrigerator at the same time.

Salads

Dellwood Salad

This is an all-time great recipe. It is absolutely delicious and can be changed a multitude of ways. Some suggestions are listed (under variations) but let your imagination go wild as you can hardly go wrong. This is also an excellent main course, served hot or cold.

5 cups cooked turkey pieces
3 celery stalks, thinly sliced
1 large can water chestnuts, sliced
1 can (16-ounce) pineapple tidbits,
**   drained**
1 bunch grapes, sliced (about 2 cups)

1½ to 2 cups mayonnaise (1/2 mayonnaise
**   and 1/2 yogurt is good)**
1 to 2 tablespoons curry powder
salt and pepper to taste
1 cup slivered almonds (sauté in
**   2 tablespoons butter and drain)**

1. Mix all ingredients, except almonds, and serve on bed of lettuce.
2. Garnish with almonds.

Variations

1. Omit grapes, pile salad into halves of papaya and bake 20 minutes at 325 degrees. Serve hot.
2. Same as above but do not bake.
3. Omit grapes, pile salad into hollowed green peppers and bake 30 minutes at 350 degrees. Serve hot.
4. Omit fruit, add hard-boiled eggs and stuff into medium-sized tomatoes.
5. Add 1 cup chopped unpeeled apple (any kind) and 1/2 cup raisins.
6. Omit almonds, add 1 cup chopped dates and 1 cup salted peanuts.
7. Use fresh pineapple, and serve the salad in hollowed-out pineapple shells (drain the shells very well before using).
8. Other fruit suggestions: bananas, sliced kiwi, strawberries, chopped papaya, and mandarin oranges.
9. Pine nuts are an expensive but delicious garnish to replace almonds. They need to be sautéd. Cashews are also good.
10. Omit the fruit and add fresh pea pods.
11. Serving idea: pack salad tightly into large bowl or mold and invert onto a large platter. Garnish with lettuce leaves. This is great for a buffet.

Lai Nani Fruit Salad

2 cups cooked turkey pieces
1 can (20-ounce) pineapple chunks, drained
1 red apple, chopped
2 oranges, peeled and chopped
2 bananas, peeled and sliced
1/4 cup coarsely chopped pecans or walnuts

1. Mix turkey and drained pineapple with dressing. Refrigerate for several hours or overnight.

2. Add apple, oranges, bananas and nuts. Toss well.

3. Serve in lettuce-lined bowl.

Dressing

1 package (3-ounce) softened cream cheese
1 can (10¾-ounce) cream of chicken soup
1½ teaspoons ground ginger
2 tablespoons grated orange peel (fresh is best)
2 tablespoons lemon juice (fresh is best)

Combine all ingredients in blender or food processor and blend well.

Layered Turkey Salad

3 cups cooked turkey pieces
1 small head Napa cabbage or iceberg lettuce, shredded
1/2 pound fresh mushrooms, sliced
1 small purple onion, chopped
1 package (10-ounce) frozen peas, thawed and drained
1 cucumber, chopped
1 cup cherry tomatoes, halved

Dressing

1½ cups mayonnaise
1½ tablespoons Dijon mustard
1 teaspoon sugar
3/4 teaspoon tarragon
1/2 teaspoon dried basil
1/4 teaspoon pepper
salt to taste

1. Combine dressing ingredients. Cover and refrigerate.

2. Arrange cabbage or lettuce in bottom of 3-quart glass bowl.

3. Top with layers of mushrooms, turkey, onion, peas, and cucumber.

4. Spread dressing evenly over top of salad and garnish with cherry tomato halves.

5. Cover lightly and chill at least 4 hours or overnight.

Turkey Salad with Peaches

4 cups cooked turkey pieces (white meat is best)
1 can (1 pound 13 ounces) sliced peaches
1/4 cup tarragon wine vinegar
1 tablespoon vegetable oil
1 cup thinly sliced celery
1/4 cup finely chopped green onion
1 cup sliced almonds, lightly toasted (325 degree oven for 10 minutes)
2/3 cup mayonnaise
1/2 teaspoon grated lemon peel
1/8 teaspoon Tabasco® sauce
crisp lettuce leaves

1. Drain peaches very well. Put into deep bowl or jar.

2. Combine vinegar and oil and pour over peaches, marinating at least 3 hours or overnight.

3. Combine turkey, celery, onion and almonds. Set aside

4. Combine mayonnaise, lemon peel, Tabasco® sauce, and the marinade which has been drained off the peaches.

5. Stir dressing into turkey mixture.

6. Spoon salad onto plates lined with lettuce leaves.

7. Garnish each salad with peach slices.

Turkey and Dill Salad

Serves 4

2 cups turkey pieces
1 cup chopped celery
1 cup frozen peas, thawed and drained
1/2 cup chopped green onions
   (tops included)
3 hard-cooked eggs, chopped
1 tablespoon dill weed
salt and pepper to taste
1/2 cup mayonnaise and 1/2 cup
   sour cream, combined

Combine all ingredients and chill well.

Turkey Pecan Salad

Serves 6

4 cups cooked turkey pieces
   (white meat is best)
1/2 cup chopped pecans, toasted
   (325 degrees for 10 minutes)
2 cups diced celery
1/2 cup sliced fresh mushrooms
6 slices cooked bacon, drained
   and crumbled
1 cup mayonnaise
1 cup sour cream
1½ teaspoons salt
dash pepper
1½ tablespoons lemon juice

1. Combine turkey, celery, mushrooms, pecans and bacon.

2. Blend mayonnaise with remaining ingredients.

3. Add to turkey mixture and toss.

4. Add extra salt and pepper, if desired.

5. Chill and serve on crisp greens.

Variation:

Omit celery, mushrooms and bacon. Add:
   2 avocados, chopped
   2 oranges, cut into bite-sized pieces
   1/2 cup raisins
   1¼ teaspoons curry powder, added to
      mayonnaise

Taco Salad

1½ pounds ground turkey
1 can (15-ounce) chili beans
3/4 teaspoon seasoning salt
1 teaspoon chili powder
1 medium head lettuce, torn into pieces
3 tomatoes, cut into wedges
1 cup shredded Cheddar cheese
1 large avocado, chopped
1 medium onion, chopped
1 can (2½-ounce) sliced black olives
1 package tortilla chips, crumbled
French or Italian salad dressing
taco sauce

1. In large skillet, brown turkey.
2. Add chili beans, seasoning salt, and chili powder. Cover and simmer about 10 minutes.
3. In large salad bowl, place lettuce, tomatoes, cheese, avocado, onion, and olives.
4. Add turkey mixture and tortilla chips and toss gently with dressing.
5. Pass the taco sauce.

Turkey and Vegetable Salad

6 cups cooked turkey pieces

3 large new potatoes, peeled, cooked, and cut into cubes

3 large carrots, peeled, cooked, and cut into cubes

6 hard-cooked eggs

1 package (10-ounce) frozen peas, thawed

2 cups chopped dill pickles (6 to 8 large)

1 bunch green onions, thinly sliced (tops included)

1/3 cup finely chopped parsley

paprika as garnish

Dressing

3/4 cup mayonnaise

3/4 cup sour cream

1 tablespoon Dijon mustard

1½ teaspoon salt

1/4 teaspoon pepper

3 tablespoons lime or lemon juice

1. Combine all dressing ingredients.

2. Combine all salad ingredients except 2 hard-cooked eggs.

3. Add dressing and mix well. Cover and chill thoroughly.

4. Garnish with 2 hard-cooked eggs, sliced, and sprinkle with paprika. You may add other garnishes also, such as cherry tomatoes, olives, watercress or lettuce.

This salad will keep about four days in refrigerator before serving.

Barbara's Turkey Rice Salad

Serves 6

3 cups cooked turkey pieces
 (white meat is best)
1½ cups cooked rice
3 green onions, chopped (tops included)
1 teaspoon curry powder
2 tablespoons vinegar (or lemon juice)
salt to taste
1/4 cup chopped green pepper
1 cup chopped celery
1 cup mayonnaise (or try half mayonnaise
 and half sour cream)
chutney as condiment
lettuce leaves

1. Combine rice, onion, curry, vinegar and salt. Cover and refrigerate overnight.
2. Add rest of ingredients, except chutney and lettuce, to rice mixture.
3. Serve on lettuce leaves with chutney on the side.

Variations

1. Add 1/2 cup toasted almond slivers to basic recipe and reserve a few for garnish.
2. Add 1 jar marinated artichoke hearts (drained) and 1/2 cup pimiento-stuffed olives (sliced) to basic recipe.
3. In place of regular rice, use chicken-flavored rice or 1 package (8 ounce) chicken-flavored Rice-A-Roni (cook according to package directions).
4. Add 1 cup sliced cauliflower and 1/2 cup sliced radishes to basic recipe.
5. Omit curry powder and add 1 cup chopped turkey ham to basic recipe.
6. Use 1/2 white rice and 1/2 wild rice.

Banana Turkey Skillet Salad

Serves 4

This has an unusual combination of ingredients but is delicious. Try it … you'll be delighted.

2 cups cooked turkey pieces
1 cup turkey stock
4 tablespoons butter, divided
1 cup celery, sliced diagonally
1/4 cup chopped green onions
1½ cups sliced bananas (3 medium)
2 tablespoons lemon juice
2 cups shredded iceberg lettuce
1/2 teaspoon curry powder
2 tablespoons flour

trust me!

1. Melt 2 tablespoons butter in large skillet over medium heat. Add celery and green onions and sauté until tender crisp. Remove to large bowl.
2. Add turkey to skillet, cook until hot and add to celery and onions.
3. Melt remaining 2 tablespoons butter in skillet.
4. Sprinkle sliced bananas with lemon juice, heat in skillet and add to turkey mixture.
5. Add lettuce to skillet, cover and heat until greens are wilted (2 minutes). Place on top of bananas in bowl.
6. In the same skillet, combine stock, curry powder and flour. Cook, stirring until sauce thickens and comes to a boil.
7. Add salad to skillet, toss gently and serve (or pour dressing over ingredients in the bowl and mix gently).

Turkey Pear Salad

4 cups cooked turkey pieces
1/2 cup walnuts, coarsely broken
1 tablespoon butter
4 large pears, fresh, unpeeled
lemon juice
3/4 cup mayonnaise
1/8 cup milk
1/2 teaspoon salt
3 celery stalks, thinly sliced
lettuce leaves

1. Sauté walnuts in butter over medium heat. Remove and drain on paper towel.

2. Cut 2 pears into 1/2-inch chunks. Dip into lemon juice.

3. Cut remaining pears lengthwise into thin slices. Dip into lemon juice.

4. In large bowl, mix mayonnaise, milk, salt and pepper until smooth.

5. Add walnuts, pear chunks, turkey and celery. Toss to mix well.

6. To serve, line plates with lettuce, spoon salad onto the lettuce and arrange pear slices around.

Comice pears are the most flavorful and are delicious in this salad. The red-skinned pears make the salad very pretty. Red grapes can also be added to make the salad more colorful.

Be still my heart!

45

Antipasto Turkey Mold

1 cup cooked turkey pieces
2 envelopes unflavored gelatin
1/4 cup cold water
3 cups turkey stock
1/3 cup white wine vinegar
1/2 teaspoon Tabasco® sauce
1/2 cup diced green pepper
1 can (2½-ounce) sliced black olives, drained
1 jar (2-ounce) diced pimientos, drained
1 jar (8-ounce) garbanzos, drained
lettuce or watercress
hard cooked eggs, artichoke hearts and cherry tomatoes as garnish

1. Soften gelatin in cold water. Heat stock and combine with gelatin, wine vinegar and Tabasco® sauce.

2. Chill until slightly thickened (about 1 hour).

3. Stir green pepper, olives, pimientos, garbanzos and turkey into gelatin mixture.

4. Spoon into a 2-quart ring mold.

5. Chill until set (about 6 hours). Unmold and serve on lettuce leaves.

6. Garnish with egg wedges, artichoke hearts and tomatoes.

We suggest serving a creamy herbed dressing with this salad. Also, turkey ham would be a good substitute for the turkey.

Oriental Meatball Salad

turkey meatballs (see recipe below)
1½ cups turkey stock
1 teaspoon sugar
2 tablespoons cornstarch
1 tablespoon sweet rice wine (mirin)
   or sherry

2 teaspoons soy sauce
1/2 teaspoon vinegar
1 head lettuce, very finely shredded
1/4 cup thinly sliced (on diagonal)
   green onions (tops included)
1 lemon, cut into wedges

1. Prepare turkey meatballs as directed.

2. While meatballs bake, prepare brown sauce by combining sugar and cornstarch in small pan. Mix in mirin, soy sauce, vinegar and stock. Stir until smooth.

3. Cook over medium heat, stirring constantly until mixture boils and thickens. Keep warm.

4. Spread shredded lettuce on serving plate, spoon hot meatballs on top. Sprinkle with green onions and garnish with lemon wedges. Serve immediately and pass the warm brown sauce.

Turkey Meatballs

1 pound ground turkey
1 egg, slightly beaten
1/3 cup chopped green onions
1½ teaspoons sesame oil
4 teaspoons soy sauce
2 tablespoons mirin or sherry
1/4 cup fine dry bread crumbs
1 can (8-ounce) water chestnuts,
   drained and chopped

1. Mix all ingredients together very well. Cover and chill 2 hours or until mixture is firm.

2. Shape into 1-inch balls and place about 1½ inches apart on two greased shallow-rimmed baking sheets.

3. Bake in 350 degree oven for 15 to 20 minutes.

Kirkpatrick's Spinach Salad

Serves 8

2 cups cooked turkey pieces
2 pounds spinach greens
1 small purple onion, thinly sliced into rings
1/2 pound bacon, cooked, drained and crumbled
1 cup alfalfa sprouts
1/2 cup almond slivers (or salted sunflower seeds)
1/2 cup cubed Cheddar cheese
1/2 cup cubed Jack cheese
1/2 cup raisins

1. Prepare dressing (see below).
2. Marinate turkey pieces and onion rings in Kirkpatrick's dressing several hours.
3. Combine remaining salad ingredients. Add dressing, turkey and onion and toss well.

Kirkpatrick's Curry Dressing
Combine the following:

1/2 cup vegetable oil
1/3 cup red wine vinegar
1 clove garlic, minced
2 tablespoons brown sugar
1 tablespoon curry powder
1 teaspoon soy sauce
2 tablespoons chopped green onions
    (or chives)

Jamie's Favorite

5 cups cooked turkey pieces (white meat is best)
1½ cups sliced celery
3 green onions, sliced (tops included)
1/2 cup slivered almonds, toasted (bake 325 degrees for 10 minutes)
3/4 cup of your favorite Italian salad dressing
lettuce leaves

1. Combine all the ingredients except lettuce and chill well.
2. Serve on lettuce leaves.

Variations

1. Arrange avocado slices (dipped in lemon juice) and orange slices around the salad before serving.
2. Add grapes, pineapple chunks and sliced banana (dipped in pineapple juice) to the salad.
3. Garnish the salad with sliced kiwi fruit and strawberries.
4. Stuff a tomato with the salad.
5. Stuff half a papaya, half a pineapple, or half a melon with the salad.
6. Add 1 cup sliced ripe olives to the salad.

experiment!

Julie's Cabbage Salad

Serves 4

1 cup cooked turkey pieces
1 head cabbage, coarsely shredded
4 green onions, chopped
1 package Top Ramen® noodles,
    oriental flavor
2 tablespoons sesame seeds
1/2 cup slivered almonds, toasted
    (bake at 325 degrees for 10 minutes)

Dressing

2 tablespoons sugar
1/2 cup vegetable oil
3 tablespoons vinegar (rice wine
    vinegar is best)
1/2 package seasoning from Top Ramen®
1 teaspoon salt
1/2 teaspoon pepper

1. Combine dressing ingredients.

2. Combine turkey, cabbage and onion.

3. Toss with dressing and refrigerate 4 to 6 hours before serving.

4. Just before serving, add noodles, seeds and almonds.

Hot Turkey Salad

Serves 6

2 cups cooked turkey pieces
2 cups thinly sliced celery
1 cup croutons
1 cup mayonnaise (1/2 mayonnaise and
    1/2 plain yogurt is good)
1/2 cup chopped or slivered almonds
    (sauté in butter until golden and
    drain on paper towel)
2 tablespoons lemon juice
2 green onions, finely chopped
1/2 teaspoon salt
1/2 cup shredded Cheddar or
    Swiss cheese
1 cup crushed potato chips.

1. Mix all ingredients except cheese and potato chips.

2. Spoon into 2 quart casserole.

3. Sprinkle with cheese and potato chips.

4. Bake uncovered 20 - 30 minutes at 350 degrees.

trust me!

Becky's Marinated Salad

Serves 6

This salad is so pretty we suggest serving it in a glass bowl. It is also nice because it can easily be made as large or as small as you want.

2 cups cooked turkey pieces
1 bunch broccoli, flowers only
1 head cauliflower, flowers only
1 box cherry tomatoes
1 purple onion, sliced into thin rings
1 cup cubed Jack cheese (Cheddar
**   cheese is also good)**
Italian dressing (any favorite)

Mix all ingredients together and marinate at least 3 hours before serving. It can be made the night before, but wait until morning to add the cheese.

Variations

1. This salad is good using turkey ham instead of regular turkey.
2. Sliced carrots and celery are a good addition to this salad.
3. Use Swiss cheese, if you like, and add slivers of salami.
4. Toss in some pitted black olives.

Easy Antipasto Salad

Serves 6

1 cup cooked turkey pieces
**   (or turkey ham pieces)**
1 jar (11-ounce) pickled mixed
**   vegetables, drained**
1 can (4-ounce) whole mushrooms,
**   drained**
1 jar (6-ounce) marinated artichoke
**   hearts, including liquid**
1 jar (8-ounce) tomato sauce
1/2 teaspoon dry basil
crisp lettuce leaves

1. Cut pickled vegetables into bite-sized pieces and combine with mushrooms and olives.
2. Cut artichokes lengthwise into 2 or 3 pieces.
3. Add artichokes and their marinade to the vegetables.
3. Stir in tomato sauce and basil.
4. Distribute turkey over top and mix gently.
5. Cover and chill at least overnight.
6. Serve on individual lettuce leaves.

If you like anchovies, use them for garnish.

Sesame Turkey Salad with Pea Pods

2 cups cooked turkey pieces
1/2 pound fresh Chinese pea pods
   (or 10-ounce package frozen)
1/2 pound bean sprouts
1/4 cup green onions, sliced on diagonal

Dressing

1/2 cup toasted sesame seeds
   (toast in 325 degree oven for
   10 minutes, stir often)
1/2 cup vegetable oil
3 cloves garlic, minced or pressed
3 tablespoons lemon juice
1½ tablespoon soy sauce
1½ tablespoon white wine vinegar
2 tablespoons fresh ginger,
   finely minced

1. Combine all dressing ingredients. Cover and refrigerate.

2. Remove ends and strings from pea pods. Cut large pods in half.

3. Steam pea pods until tender crisp.

4. Combine pea pods, bean sprouts and turkey.

5. Pour dressing over and mix gently.

6. Top with sliced green onions.

This salad garnished with grapes and sliced cantaloupe makes a light and yummy dinner.

52

Curried Spinach Salad

2 cups cooked turkey pieces (white meat is best)
2 pounds spinach, clean and torn
3 red or golden delicious apples, unpeeled, cored and diced
2/3 cup dry roasted peanuts
1/2 cup golden raisins
1/3 cup thinly sliced green onions
2 tablespoons sesame seeds
curry dressing (see below)

Combine all ingredients and toss with dressing.

Curry Dressing

1 teaspoon curry
1 teaspoon salt
1 teaspoon dry mustard
1/2 cup white wine vinegar
2/3 cup vegetable oil
1 tablespoon chopped chutney
1/4 teaspoon Tabasco® sauce

1. Combine ingredients and shake or stir well.
2. Let stand 2 hours at room temperature.

Sandwiches

Classic Turkey Sandwich

Serves 2

lots of thinly sliced turkey (white meat is best)
plenty of mayonnaise
salt to taste
crisp lettuce leaves
fresh white bread

Spread the bread with mayonnaise, layer with lots of turkey, top with lettuce, salt to taste, add the top piece of bread and enjoy!

Variations

1. Sourdough bread is great instead of white. Many prefer a whole grain bread as well. There are wonderful breads on the market now, so try a variety.

2. Omit the mayonnaise and use softened cream cheese and cranberry sauce.

3. Add tomato slices and slices of your favorite cheese.

4. Omit the mayonnaise and add ginger marmalade and cream cheese.

5. Stuffing and cranberries in place of or along with turkey is terrific.

6. Sprouts are good in place of lettuce.

7. Add some cooked and drained bacon slices and toast the bread.

8. Add thinly sliced pears or apples.

9. Add your favorite kind of pickle (bread and butter pickles are especially good).

Hot Pastrami Sandwich

**thinly sliced turkey pastrami (about
   1½ pounds)
1 can (16-ounce) sauerkraut, well drained
12 slices Swiss cheese
mayonnaise
softened butter
12 large slices dark rye bread**

1. Spread one side of each bread slice with mayonnaise.
2. On six bread slices, layer turkey, sauerkraut and cheese.
3. Top with remaining bread slices, mayonnaise side down.
4. Spread top bread slice evenly with softened butter and place butter side down on medium heated skillet.
5. Butter top of other bread slice.
6. Grill slowly on each side until golden brown.

Variations

1. This can be made with turkey ham or turkey breast. All are good. You can also vary the cheese to your taste. It's good served with potato chips and dill pickles.
2. Omit the sauerkraut, add tomato slices and thinly sliced onion rings.
3. Use horseradish mustard instead of mayonnaise.

Mexican Turkey Sandwich

Serves 2

**1 cup finely chopped cooked
    turkey pieces**
1/4 cup finely chopped celery
**1 large green onion, chopped
    (tops included)**
1 tablespoon chopped green chiles
1 to 2 teaspoons chili powder
1/4 teaspoon cumin
2 tablespoons mayonnaise
2 tablespoons sour cream
**1/2 cup grated Swiss cheese (Cheddar
    is also good)**
**2 large slices sourdough bread
    (or 2 English muffins)**
1/2 cup chopped tomato
1/2 cup chopped avocado

1. Combine the first eight ingredients.
2. Toast the bread or muffins.
3. Spread bread generously with turkey mixture.
4. Top with cheese.
5. Bake 350 degrees for 15 minutes or until cheese melts.
6. Garnish with tomato and avocado.

Kieburtz-Kaiser

Serves 2

1 cup cooked turkey pieces
2 stalks celery, chopped
1 cup seedless grapes, cut in half
**1/2 cup toasted almonds (bake
    325 degrees for 10 minutes)**
1/2 cup mayonnaise
lettuce
1/4 cup butter
2 Kaiser rolls

1. Mix turkey, celery, grapes, almonds and mayonnaise together.
2. Butter halves of rolls.
3. Spread half the roll with the turkey mixture and top with lettuce and the other half of the roll.

Variations

1. Use only 1/2 cup grapes; add 1/2 cup crushed pineapple (drained).
2. Add other fruits such as papaya, mandarin oranges, apple or pear.
3. Omit grapes and add chopped onions and mushrooms.

Curried Turkey Salad

Serves 4

2 cups cooked turkey pieces
1/2 cup chopped celery
1/2 cup mayonnaise
2 tablespoons lemon juice
   (or 1 tablespoon grated lemon peel)
1½ teaspoon curry powder
1/2 cup coarsely chopped chutney
raisins and chopped nuts
   (peanuts or cashews)
4 sourdough or French rolls

1. Combine turkey, celery, mayonnaise, lemon juice, curry powder, and chutney. Chill.

2. Cut 1/2-inch slice from top of rolls and hollow out center of bottom, leaving 1/2-inch shell.

3. Fill with salad mixture, sprinkle with raisins and nuts.

4. Replace top. Wrap well and chill.

These make great picnic rolls as they must be done ahead of time.

Curried Turkey Sandwich

Serves 4

2 cups cooked turkey pieces
1/2 cup mayonnaise
1/2 teaspoon garlic salt
1/2 teaspoon prepared mustard
1 teaspoon curry powder
   (more if you like)
2 tablespoons chutney, chopped
2/3 cup chopped celery
2 to 3 green onions, chopped
   (tops included)
1 small apple, chopped (about 1 cup)
1/4 cup cashew nuts, coarsely chopped
4 Pita bread rounds

Combine all ingredients and serve in Pita bread.

Turkey and Asparagus

Serves 4

**thinly sliced turkey breast
    (about 1 pound)
1 can (10¾-ounce) condensed cream
    of mushroom soup
1/4 cup milk
4 to 5 drops Tabasco® sauce
1 can (16-ounce) asparagus spears,
    well drained
3 hard-cooked eggs, sliced
1/4 cup grated Parmesan cheese
paprika
4 English muffins, split and toasted**

1. Blend soup, milk and Tabasco® sauce. Cook and stir over medium heat until smooth.
2. Place muffin halves on baking sheet and toast under broiler.
3. Top each muffin half with turkey, asparagus and egg slices.
4. Spoon soup mixture over.
5. Sprinkle with cheese and paprika.
6. Broil until bubbly and lightly browned. Serve hot.

This would also be very good if garnished with black olives or mushrooms.

Turkey Divan

Serves 6

**thinly sliced turkey breast
    (about 1½ pounds)
3/4 cup mayonnaise
1/4 cup grated Parmesan cheese
1 teaspoon dry mustard
2 tablespoons milk
1/4 cup chopped green onions
6 slices Swiss or Jack cheese
1 package (10-ounce) frozen broccoli
    spears, thawed and drained
3 (6-inch) hard rolls, split**

1. In a small bowl, combine mayonnaise, Parmesan cheese, mustard, milk and green onions.
2. Arrange roll halves in shallow baking dish.
3. Spread thin layer of mayonnaise mixture on each roll half.
4. Layer turkey, cheese and broccoli on rolls.
5. Spoon on mayonnaise mixture.
6. Bake uncovered, 15 to 20 minutes at 400 degrees. Serve hot.

try it! you'll like... it!

Peanutty Turkey Pocket

Serves 2

2 cups cooked turkey pieces
1/2 cup turkey stock
2 tablespoons soy sauce
1 tablespoon cornstarch
1/4 teaspoon garlic powder
dash of hot sauce or curry powder
  to taste
1/2 cup chopped red or green
  bell pepper
1/4 cup chopped peanuts
2 Pita bread rounds, halved

1. Blend stock with soy sauce, cornstarch, and seasonings; cook until thickened and bubbly.

2. Add chopped pepper and peanuts and simmer over low heat until peppers are tender crisp.

3. Add turkey and heat through.

4. Spoon into warmed Pita pockets.

For a change, try adding 1/4 cup crushed pineapple, well drained, or 1/4 cup chopped mandarin oranges.

Turkey Pizza Pockets

Serves 6

1 pound ground turkey
2 teaspoons vegetable oil
1/2 cup chopped onion
2 cloves garlic, minced
1 teaspoon Italian seasoning
1/2 teaspoon salt
1 can (8-ounce) tomato sauce
1 can (2½-ounce) sliced black olives,
  drained
6 Pita bread rounds
1½ cups shredded lettuce
1 large tomato, chopped
1 cup shredded Mozzarella cheese

1. Brown turkey in oil along with onion and garlic. Drain excess fat.

2. Stir in Italian seasoning, salt, tomato sauce and olives. Cook 5 minutes.

3. Cut pocket breads in half and open to form pockets.

4. Fill with lettuce, meat mixture, tomato, and cheese.

Turkey Pineapple

Serves 4

**thinly sliced turkey breast
(about 1 pound)
1 cup Ricotta cheese
salt to taste
4 canned pineapple rings, drained
(or drained crushed pineapple)
8 slices whole wheat bread, toasted**

1. Butter the toasted bread and spread each slice with cheese.
2. On 4 slices of bread, add pineapple rings and pile high with turkey.
3. Top with remaining bread slices and serve.

Hawaiian Sandwich

Serves 6

**2 cups cooked turkey pieces,
finely chopped
1 can (4-ounce) diced water chestnuts
1 cup diced celery
1/2 cup finely chopped almonds
or cashews
1/2 cup seedless grapes, cut in half
1 cup mayonnaise (or half mayonnaise and half sour cream)
1/2 teaspoon curry
1 teaspoon soy sauce
lettuce leaves
fresh pineapple spears for garnish
12 slices white bread (sourdough
is also good)**

1. Blend all ingredients together except lettuce, pineapple and bread.
2. Butter bread and spread filling on 6 slices.
3. Top with lettuce leaf and remaining bread slices.
4. Garnish with pineapple spears.

To serve open style, split and butter 6 English muffins. Toast them under the broiler and mound mixture onto muffins and serve.

Ginger Turkey Pockets

Serves 4

3 cups cooked turkey pieces
3/4 cup turkey stock
1 tablespoon brown sugar
1 tablespoon cornstarch
1/4 cup ketchup
1/2 cup soy sauce
1 tablespoon lemon juice
1 clove garlic, minced
1/4 teaspoon ground ginger
1 package (10-ounce) frozen
**   Chinese vegetables**
3 tablespoons chopped green onion
4 Pita bread rounds, halved

1. Combine sugar and cornstarch. Stir in stock, ketchup, soy sauce, lemon juice, garlic and ginger. Cook until thick.

2. Stir in vegetables and onion. Cook until tender crisp.

3. Stir in turkey and heat through.

4. Spoon hot mixture into warmed Pita pockets.

Turkey and Sprouts

Serves 4

3 cups cooked turkey pieces
1/2 cup sliced water chestnuts
1/2 cup chopped green onion
1/2 cup coarsely chopped cashew nuts
3/4 cup mayonnaise
1/2 cup sliced green grapes
2 cups sprouts
4 Pita bread rounds, halved

1. Mix all ingredients together except sprouts.

2. Lightly mayonnaise inside Pita rounds.

3. Pile sprouts into Pita bread, top with filling, and serve.

Greek Pita Pockets

Serves 6

**1 pound ground turkey or
    turkey sausage
2 tablespoons lemon juice
pinch of cinnamon
pinch of nutmeg
1 clove garlic, finely minced
2 tablespoons chopped fresh mint
    (1 or 2 tablespoons dried)
1/2 teaspoon oregano
1 tablespoon chopped parsley
1 onion, chopped
1/2 cup chopped deli-style pickles
1 large tomato, peeled and cubed
6 Pita breads, heated
1 cup plain yogurt (optional)**

1. Shape meat into tiny meatballs, brown lightly in large skillet and drain.

2. Stir in lemon juice, seasonings, onion, pickle and tomatoes.

3. Cover tightly and simmer 2 to 3 minutes or until vegetables are tender crisp.

4. Split the heated Pita bread and fill the pockets with the meat and vegetable mixture.

5. Spoon on yogurt, if desired.

Club Sandwich

Serves 4

**thinly sliced turkey breast
    (about 1 pound)
1/2 cup mayonnaise
1/2 cup cranberry sauce
3 medium tomatoes, sliced
sprouts or lettuce
thinly sliced turkey ham (about 1 pound)
1/2 cup sour cream
12 slices Swiss cheese
12 slices white bread, toasted**

1. Spread 4 slices of toast with mayonnaise. Add cranberry sauce, turkey, tomato and lettuce (or sprouts).

2. Spread 4 slices of toast with mayonnaise and top first layers.

3. Spread opposite sides of second toast slices with sour cream.

4. Layer ham and cheese onto second slices.

5. Spread remaining toast slices with sour cream and top sandwiches.

6. Secure with toothpicks and slice into quarters.

Cooked, drained bacon slices are a good addition.

Oriental Sandwich

Serves 8

1 small uncooked turkey breast
(about 2 to 3 pounds)
1/4 cup sherry
1/4 cup honey
1/2 cup soy sauce
1/4 teaspoon seasoning salt
1/4 teaspoon cinnamon
8 seeded rolls of your choice
prepared mustard

1. Combine sherry, honey, soy sauce, seasoning salt and cinnamon. Marinate turkey for 6 or more hours.

2. Drain turkey and place in foil-lined roasting pan.

3. Roast turkey breast for 1 hour at 350 degrees.

4. Slice thinly against grain of meat.

5. Slice rolls in half, spread with mustard and pile high with turkey. Top with other half of roll and serve.

Open-Faced Turkey Melt

Serves 6

thinly sliced turkey breast
(about 1½ pounds)
12 slices cooked bacon
6 large tomato slices
(or 12 medium slices)
12 cheese slices (American, Cheddar or Swiss)
mayonnaise
6 slices white or whole wheat bread

1. Spread each bread slice with mayonnaise.

2. Layer turkey, bacon and tomato onto bread. Top with cheese.

3. Bake 15 minutes at 350 degrees until hot and cheese is melted.

Sautéed onion rings would be a good addition.

Turkey - Chile Monte Cristo

Serves 4

For best results, prepare the filling of this sandwich at least 1 hour ahead of time to let the flavors blend.

1 cup cooked turkey pieces, chopped
1/4 cup chopped celery
1/4 cup minced onion
1/4 cup chopped green pepper
1/4 cup chopped green chiles
1/2 teaspoon chile powder
1/4 cup mayonnaise
salt to taste
4 slices cheese (Jack, Swiss or Cheddar)
8 slices firm-textured bread
2 eggs
1/4 cup milk
2 tablespoons butter

Aye yi-yi-yi!

1. Mix together the turkey, celery, onion, green peppers, green chiles, chile powder and mayonnaise. Add salt to taste.

2. Spread mixture on half the bread slices.

3. Top with cheese slices and then with remaining bread slices.

4. Beat eggs and milk together.

5. Dip both sides of sandwiches in egg mixture and fry over medium heat in butter.

6. Turn sandwiches once until golden brown on both sides.

This is also good if you add a slice of ham to the sandwiches and serve with grape jelly.

Monte Cristo

thinly sliced turkey breast
(about 1 pound)
thinly sliced turkey ham (about
1 pound)
butter
Dijon mustard
3 whole tomatoes, sliced thin
(use firm tomatoes)

6 slices Swiss or Jack cheese
4 eggs, beaten well
1/2 cup milk
1/2 teaspoon salt
1/4 teaspoon paprika
12 slices white bread (day-old is best)

1. Spread bread with thin layer of butter and Dijon mustard.
2. On 6 slices, layer turkey, ham, tomatoes and cheese. Top with other 6 slices of bread.
3. Coat bottom of skillet with butter and heat.
4. Combine eggs, milk, salt and paprika and mix well.
5. Dip both sides of sandwiches into egg mixture and fry until golden brown.
6. Turn sandwiches over and brown other side.

This is very good served with little kebabs of fresh strawberries, cantaloupe, and pineapple.

Variations

1. Omit the mustard and tomatoes and spread the bread with jellied cranberry sauce or with pineapple or apricot preserves.
2. Omit the mustard and add 2 tablespoons chopped onions and 1 cup sliced fresh mushrooms.
3. Add 2 tablespoons Parmesan cheese to egg mixture.

Barbequed Turkey Sandwich

Serves 4

2 cups cooked turkey pieces
2 tablespoons butter
1 onion, sliced
1 stalk celery, chopped
1 green pepper, diced
salt and pepper to taste
1/2 teaspoon paprika
1 tablespoon Worcestershire sauce
1 tablespoon lemon juice
2 tablespoons cider vinegar
1/4 cup brown sugar
1 bottle (12-ounce) chili sauce
1 tablespoon mustard
4 hamburger buns

1. In large skillet, sauté onion, celery and green pepper in butter. Season with salt, pepper and paprika.

2. Add the rest of the ingredients, except turkey and hamburger buns, and simmer 30 minutes.

3. Add turkey and heat thoroughly in sauce.

4. Toast the buns and spoon the turkey mixture over.

Chuck's Sit Sandwich

Serves 6

This sandwich is a "smashing success" . . . in more ways than one. It's a great traveler.

thinly sliced turkey breast (about 1/2 pound)
thinly sliced salami (about 3 ounces)
1/4 pound cheese slices (any kind)
1 jar marinated artichoke hearts, reserve liquid
1/2 cup mayonnaise
1 purple onion, thinly sliced
3 large tomatoes, sliced
1 can (2½-ounce) sliced ripe olives, drained
1 large round loaf French bread

1. Cut loaf of bread in half horizontally and hollow out the soft bread from both halves, leaving a shell about 3/4-inch thick. Reserve soft bread for another use.

2. In small bowl, combine artichoke liquid with mayonnaise and spread onto bread shells.

3. In bottom half, layer ingredients until mounded high. Be sure to begin and end with tomatoes and also put them in the center.

4. Place top half of bread over mound of ingredients. Wrap entire loaf with plastic wrap. This must be assembled at least two hours before serving but can be assembled up to 8 hours before serving. Refrigerate.

5. Before serving, place sandwich (wrapped in plastic) on a hard surface and SIT ON IT! This smashes the ingredients together and makes it easy to serve. Do not omit this step . . . strange as it seems . . . as this step is what makes the sandwich delicious. Slice the loaf into wedges to serve. Have fun!

Cutlets

Turkey Cutlets

Turkey Cutlets are a relatively new concept which will surprise and delight you. They are slices of uncooked turkey breast which have been cut across the grain perpendicular to the breast bone. They are extremely versatile, low in fat and very economical. They can be used in place of pork, veal, or chicken. They can be sautéed, simmered, baked or grilled. They can be pounded thin, stuffed or rolled. They are the perfect choice for a dinner party because they are so elegant when cooked in wine or a rich sauce. They are an excellent choice for a simple family meal as they can be quickly prepared. They are a dieter's choice because of their low-fat-to-protein ratio. Their possibilities are limitless. Cutlets can be used for any occasion during any season.

Several of our cutlet recipes call for butter and/or cream. We feel these greatly enhance the flavor, and considering the leanness of the cutlet, the proportion of fat to meat is very small. However, if you prefer, you can always substitute with low-fat margarine or richer-flavored turkey stock for butter and low-fat evaporated milk or skim milk with powdered milk added for cream.

Most meat markets are now selling cutlets. However, you can easily prepare your own at a considerable savings as is illustrated in the diagram. It is important to select a large-breasted bird, preferably one that has not been pre-basted. For best results, start with a bird that has only partially thawed and use a very sharp knife.

How To Carve Cutlets

For best results, start with a large breasted bird that has only partially thawed. This makes it easier to slice. Use a carving board and a very sharp knife.

1. Place the breast before you on the carving board with the breast bone facing you. Place the tip of the knife along one side of the breast bone and begin cutting through the skin as close to the bone as possible, pulling the meat away as you cut.

2. Continue cutting and pulling along the breast bone and the ribs until the breast section falls free. Repeat on the other side.

3. Remove the skin by using the knife to cut through the membrane between the meat and the skin.

4. Cut the cutlets across the grain (perpendicular to the breast bone) in the width you desire. The meat will separate slightly but don't worry. Just reshape the cutlet and it will hold together as it cooks.

Use the large pieces for cutlets and the smaller ones for recipes calling for uncooked turkey pieces. Save the skin and the breast bone for stock (See page 19).

Basic Turkey Cutlet

Serves 4

8 turkey cutlets
seasoned flour
**   (combine 1 cup flour, 2 teaspoons salt, and 1/2 teaspoon pepper)**
1/4 cup butter
sauce of your choice

1. Coat turkey in seasoned flour and sauté in butter until lightly browned. Do not overcook (turkey will get tough).
2. Place turkey in shallow baking dish.
3. Cover with the sauce of your choice.
4. Bake 350 degrees for about 30 minutes.

Be sure to read the introduction to the cutlet section of this cookbook. It will give you low-calorie ideas on how to cook cutlets.

Pat's Gravy

2 cups richer-flavored turkey stock
1/4 cup butter
1/4 cup flour
1/3 cup dry sherry
salt and pepper to taste

1. Melt butter in sauce pan. Add flour, stirring well with whisk until blended. Cook two minutes.
2. Add stock slowly and stir until gravy is thickened.
3. Add sherry and blend well. Salt and pepper to taste. Pour over cutlets and bake.

Basic Turkey Cutlet, continued

Easy Sweet and Sour Sauce

1/2 cup Red Russian dressing of
 your choice
1/2 envelope onion soup mix
3/4 cup pineapple-apricot jam
1 teaspoon dry mustard

Combine all ingredients and heat slowly. Pour over cutlets and serve.

Pear Sauce

3/4 teaspoon crumbled basil leaves
1/3 cup grated Parmesan cheese
1/3 cup almonds
2 medium firm-ripe pears, sliced
2/3 cup dry white wine
salt to taste

1. In place of seasoned flour, dredge the cutlets in combination of basil and Parmesan cheese. Sauté in butter and remove to baking dish.
2. In same pan, add almonds and stir until golden. Remove and set aside.
3. Add pears and wine to pan. Cook, uncovered, until most of liquid is absorbed. Turn the fruit often.
4. Pour pears over cutlets, sprinkle with almonds, and bake.

White Sauce

1/4 cup butter
1/4 cup flour
2 cups milk
salt and pepper to taste

1. Melt butter in sauce pan. Add flour, stirring well with whisk until blended. Cook two minutes.
2. Add milk slowly; whisk until sauce is thickened. Bring sauce to a boil, stirring constantly until thickened.
3. Add salt and pepper to taste. Pour over cutlets and bake.

Veloute' Sauce

2 cups richer-flavored turkey stock
1/4 cup butter
1/4 cup flour
salt and pepper to taste

1. Melt butter in sauce pan. Add flour, stirring well with whisk until blended. Cook two minutes.
2. Add stock slowly; stir until sauce is thickened.
3. Add salt and pepper to taste. Pour over cutlets and bake.

Basic Turkey Cutlet, continued

Chutney Sauce

2 tablespoons butter
1 medium apple, peeled, cored
  and diced
1 teaspoon curry powder
1/2 teaspoon cinnamon
1/4 teaspoon thyme
1/4 teaspoon ground ginger
1/4 cup Major Grey's Chutney, chopped
1 can (11-ounce) mandarin oranges,
  reserve liquid
3/4 cup seedless grapes

1. Add butter to skillet and sauté apple, curry powder, cinnamon, thyme, ginger and chutney.

2. Add liquid from oranges and cook until slightly reduced.

3. Pour over turkey and bake.

4. Just before serving, top turkey with oranges and grapes and bake an additional ten minutes.

Lime Butter Sauce

juice of one lime
1/2 cup butter
1/2 teaspoon minced chives
1/2 teaspoon dill weed

1. Add lime juice to the remaining juices in the skillet and cook over low heat until juice begins to bubble.

2. Add butter, stirring well until thickened.

3. Stir in chives and dill weed. Pour over cutlets and serve.

Paprika Sauce

1/4 cup Parmesan cheese
1 tablespoon paprika
1½ cup heavy cream (can substitute
  yogurt or richer-flavored stock)

1. Add cheese and paprika to seasoned flour to coat cutlets before browning.

2. Cover cutlets with cream and bake.

Lemon Sauce

1 teaspoon cornstarch
3/4 cup half and half, divided
2 tablespoons sherry
1 tablespoon lemon juice
1 teaspoon grated lemon peel
1/2 cup grated Swiss cheese
chopped parsley for garnish

1. Combine cornstarch with 1/4 cup half and half and stir into drippings in skillet.

2. Gradually add remaining half and half, sherry lemon juice and lemon peel.

3. When thickened, pour over turkey cutlets.

4. Cover and bake 350 degrees for 20 minutes.

5. Uncover, add cheese; bake until cheese melts.

6. Garnish with parsley.

Sour Cream and Mushroom Sauce

2 tablespoons butter
1 cup sliced fresh mushrooms
1 cup sour cream
dash paprika
1 tablespoon grated onion (you can buy
    a jar of grated onion and keep
    in the refrigerator)

1. Add butter to skillet and sauté mushrooms.
2. Gradually add sour cream, paprika, onion, and salt and pepper to taste.
3. Pour over cutlets and bake.

Tchakhokhbelli Sauce

2 tablespoons butter
1 large onion, sliced
1/4 cup sherry
1/4 cup tomato juice
1/2 cup water
1 teaspoon paprika
1 teaspoon salt
pepper to taste

1. Add butter to skillet and sauté onion.
2. Add remaining ingredients.
3. Pour over turkey and bake.

Creamy Mustard Sauce

1 cup plain yogurt
1/4 cup Dijon mustard

1. Add yogurt to skillet and stir into drippings.
2. Add mustard and stir until heated.
3. Pour over turkey and bake.

Amandine Sauce

1½ cup turkey stock
2 tablespoons lemon juice
1/2 cup sliced almonds
1/4 cup butter
2 tablespoons chopped parsley

1. Sprinkle cutlets with lemon juice before dredging with flour.
2. Reserve seasoned flour.
3. Sauté almonds in butter and drain on paper towel. Set aside. (Or bake 325 degrees for 10 minutes.)
4. Stir 3 tablespoons reserved flour into skillet drippings.
5. Gradually add turkey stock; stir until smooth.
6. Pour sauce over turkey, top with almonds and bake.
7. Garnish with parsley.

The Slender Cutlets

It seems as if someone is always on a diet. These recipes will help to make your diet more enjoyable. They contain no fat or sugar, but are still delicious, versatile, and substantial. They are for individual servings, however, you can easily make as many servings as you wish. Just remember to lengthen the cooking time for each additional cutlet.

Garlic and Rosemary

1 half-inch cutlet
garlic salt to taste
rosemary leaves to taste (fresh or dried)

Place cutlet in foil. Sprinkle with garlic salt and rosemary and wrap. Bake 350 degrees for 15 to 20 minutes.

Green Onions and Mushrooms

1 half-inch cutlet
1 tablespoon chopped green onions
3 whole mushrooms
lemon pepper to taste

Place cutlet in foil and top with green onions and mushrooms. Season with lemon pepper and wrap. Bake 350 degrees for 15 to 20 minutes.

Dijon Cutlet

1 half-inch cutlet
Dijon mustard to taste

Place cutlet in foil. Spread mustard over one side of cutlet and wrap. Bake 350 degrees for 15 to 20 minutes.

Curried Fruit Cutlet

1 half-inch cutlet
1 cup coarsely chopped fresh fruit (apples, pears, bananas, grapes, oranges, or any combination you prefer)
1/2 teaspoon curry powder
artificial sweetener
1 tablespoon water

1. Combine fruit, curry, sweetener and water in small sauce pan. Cover and cook over low heat until fruit is soft, stirring occasionally to prevent scorching.

2. Place cutlet in foil, top with fruit mixture, and wrap.

3. Bake 350 degrees for 15 to 20 minutes.

Unsweetened canned fruit could also be used. Just combine the fruit with curry and artificial sweetener, place on top of the cutlet and bake. There is no need to precook the canned fruit.

The Slender Cutlets, continued

Tomato Cutlet

> 1 half-inch cutlet
> salt and pepper to taste
> 1 slice of tomato
> basil to taste (cilantro or oregano
>   is also good)
> 1 tablespoon low-fat cottage cheese
>   (or grated Cheddar cheese)

Place cutlet in foil and season with salt and pepper. Top with tomato and sprinkle with basil. Add cottage cheese and wrap. Bake 350 degrees for 20 minutes.

Spinach and Cottage Cheese

> 1 half-inch cutlet
> 2 tablespoons chopped spinach,
>   cooked and drained
> 2 tablespoons cottage cheese
> 1 teaspoon chopped green onion
> garlic salt to taste
> salt and pepper to taste

Place cutlet in foil. Combine the remaining ingredients and place on top of the cutlet. Wrap tightly and bake 350 degrees for 15 to 20 minutes.

Pineapple Cutlet

> 1 half-inch cutlet
> salt and pepper to taste
> slice of fresh pineapple (canned
>   is also good)

Place cutlet in foil. Season with salt and pepper and top with pineapple. Wrap tightly and bake 350 degrees for 15 to 20 minutes. An orange slice would also be good.

Turkey Kiev

8 turkey cutlets, pounded thin
1/4 cup soft butter
1½ teaspoons oregano, divided
1 tablespoon chopped parsley
1/4 pound Jack cheese, cut into 8 fingers
    (1/2-inch thick by 1½-inches long)
3/4 cup bread crumbs, finely crushed
3/4 cup grated Parmesan cheese
1/2 teaspoon garlic salt
1/4 teaspoon pepper
5 tablespoons melted butter

1. Combine soft butter, 1/2 teaspoon oregano, and parsley and spread over cutlets.
2. Top each cutlet with finger of cheese and roll up, tucking ends under.
3. Combine bread crumbs, cheese, garlic salt, pepper, and remaining oregano.
4. Dip rolled cutlets in melted butter and then in combined bread crumbs.
5. Place seam side down, without sides touching, in a shallow baking dish.
6. Cover and chill at least 4 hours or overnight.
7. Bake, uncovered, at 400 degrees for 20 minutes or until turkey is done.

Variation

This is an exciting Mexican version that makes a totally different dish.

Add a whole green chili (seeds removed) along with the finger of cheese.

Pass the spicy tomato sauce, a combination of: 1 can (15-ounce) tomato sauce
                                         1/2 teaspoon cumin
                                         1/3 cup chopped green onion
                                         salt, pepper and Tabasco® sauce to taste.

Florentine Turkey Rolls

Serves 4

8 large turkey cutlets, pounded thin
3/4 cup turkey stock
1/4 cup butter
1/2 pound fresh mushrooms, thinly sliced
1/4 cup flour
1/4 teaspoon ground nutmeg
1/4 teaspoon white pepper
3/4 cup white wine
3/4 cup half & half
1 package (10-ounce) frozen chopped spinach, thawed and squeezed dry
2 cups shredded Swiss cheese, divided

1. Sauté mushrooms in butter until soft.

2. Remove from heat and stir in flour, nutmeg, and pepper.

3. Gradually stir in stock, wine and half & half until smooth.

4. Cook and stir until thickened. Set aside.

5. Mix spinach, 1 cup of the cheese and 1/4 cup of mushroom sauce.

6. Place 1/4 cup filling at one end of each cutlet and roll up tightly.

7. Place seam side down in buttered, shallow baking dish.

8. Cover with remaining sauce and top with remaining cheese.

9. Bake 350 degrees for 30 minutes.

Janet's Wiener Schnitzel

Serves 6

8 turkey cutlets, pounded thin
1 cup lemon juice (fresh is best)
salt and pepper to taste
2 eggs, beaten
2 tablespoons water
1 cup flour
1 cup bread crumbs
1/2 cup butter
lemon wedges and anchovies

1. Marinate cutlets in lemon juice for 1 hour.

2. Drain and pat dry with paper towels and sprinkle with salt and pepper.

3. Combine eggs and water. Dip cutlets in egg mixture and then in flour. Shake off excess flour.

4. Dip cutlets in bread crumbs. Shake off excess. Refrigerate at least 20 minutes.

5. Melt butter in large skillet and sauté cutlets a few minutes on each side until golden brown. Do not overcook.

6. Garnish with lemon wedges and anchovies (if desired).

Turkey, Ham and Cheese

Serves 4

6 to 8 large cutlets, pounded very thin
6 to 8 slices of Swiss or Gruyere cheese, same size as cutlets
6 to 8 thin slices of ham, same size as cutlets
1 can (10¾-ounce) cream of mushroom soup
1 cup sour cream
1/4 cup sauterne or sherry
1/4 cup melted butter
1 cup crushed Ritz crackers
1/2 pound fresh mushrooms, sliced
2 tablespoons butter

1. Place one ham and one cheese slice on each turkey cutlet and roll up.

2. Make sauce of soup, sour cream and wine. Pour into bottom of shallow baking dish.

3. Roll cutlets in melted butter, then in crackers, and place seam side down in sauce on baking dish.

4. In a skillet, briefly sauté mushrooms in butter and sprinkle over top of cutlets.

5. Cover baking dish and bake 350 degrees for 30 minutes.

6. Uncover and cook an additional 10 minutes.

Bacon - Spinach Stuffed

Serves 4

8 turkey cutlets, pounded thin
8 slices bacon, diced
1 large onion, chopped
1 package (10-ounce) frozen chopped
    spinach, thawed and squeezed dry
1 egg, slightly beaten
1/2 cup seasoned croutons,
    lightly crushed
1/2 teaspoon garlic salt
salt and pepper to taste
3 tablespoons butter
lemon wedges for garnish

1. Cook bacon in skillet until crisp. Drain on paper towel.

2. Pour off all but 2 tablespoons drippings. Add onion and sauté until golden.

3. Remove from heat and add bacon, spinach, egg, croutons and garlic salt. Blend well.

4. Place small mound of stuffing on each cutlet and roll up. Season with salt and pepper. Secure with toothpick if needed.

5. Heat butter in skillet over medium heat. Sauté cutlets on all sides until golden brown, about 10 minutes. Do not overcook. Remove toothpicks.

6. Serve with lemon wedges to squeeze over the top.

Chinese - Barbequed

Serves 4

This is a simple and delicious recipe but you must start preparation two days ahead of time.

8 large turkey cutlets (1½-inch thick)
1 teaspoon grated fresh ginger
1 teaspoon dry mustard
1 teaspoon monosodium glutamate
1 tablespoon honey
1/2 cup soy sauce
1/4 cup vegetable oil
3 cloves garlic, minced

1. Combine all ingredients (except cutlets) into bowl.

2. Let stand 24 hours at room temperature.

3. Pour over cutlets. Cover and refrigerate overnight.

4. Drain cutlets and cook quickly on barbeque grill (or under broiler), allowing about 8 minutes each side.

5. Brush turkey with marinade occasionally during cooking.

Ah- Soooo Good!

83

Jeff's Favorite Cutlets

Serves 4

8 turkey cutlets, pounded thin
1 package Stove Top Stuffing®
1/4 pound bacon

1. Prepare stuffing according to directions on box but do not cook.
2. Place mound of stuffing on each cutlet and roll up.
3. Place in buttered shallow baking dish.
4. Top each roll-up with 1/3 strip of uncooked bacon.
5. Bake 350 degrees for 30 to 45 minutes. Serve with pan juices.

This is delicious served with cranberry sauce and a fresh green vegetable.

Steve's Italian Cutlets

Serves 8

12 turkey cutlets, pounded thin
1½ cups turkey stock
salt and pepper to taste
4 cloves garlic, pressed
1 cup flour
3 tablespoons butter
3 tablespoons oil
1/2 teaspoon dried tarragon
1/2 cup dry white wine
12 slices turkey ham (or regular ham)
12 slices Mozzarella cheese

1. Sprinkle cutlets with salt and pepper and rub with garlic. Dredge lightly with flour.
2. Heat butter and oil in large frying pan. Sauté turkey until golden but do not overcook. Remove to shallow baking dish and sprinkle with tarragon.
3. Place slices of ham over cutlets.
4. Add stock to skillet and heat, scraping brown particles. Add wine and bring to boil. Pour over turkey and ham.
5. Cover and bake 30 minutes at 350 degrees.
6. About 5 minutes before serving, add cheese slices and bake uncovered until melted.

Mary's Champagne Turkey

Serves 4

8 turkey cutlets
1 cup turkey stock
3 tablespoons flour
1 teaspoon salt
1 tablespoon butter
1 tablespoon vegetable oil
2 tablespoons curacao
3/4 cup dry champagne
1 cup sliced fresh mushrooms
1 tablespoon melted butter
1/2 cup heavy cream
orange wedges and seedless grapes
      as garnish

1. Dredge cutlets in combined flour and salt.
2. Sauté cutlets in butter and oil for 5 minutes each side. Do not overcook.
3. Place cutlets in shallow baking dish. Bake uncovered for 20 minutes at 350 degrees.
4. While cutlets are baking, pour fat from skillet, and add curacao, champagne, and stock. Bring to simmer.
5. Pour sauce over turkey in baking dish. Continue cooking 10 more minutes.
6. Sauté mushrooms in melted butter. Add cream and spoon over turkey just before serving.
7. Garnish with orange wedges and grapes.

Ginger Cream Turkey

Serves 4

6 large turkey cutlets, pounded thin
3/4 cup turkey stock
seasoned flour (1/2 cup flour,
      1 teaspoon ginger, 1 teaspoon salt,
      1/4 teaspoon pepper)
1/4 cup butter
2 green onions, minced
3 tablespoons flour
1/2 cup Madeira
3/4 cup half and half
1/4 cup minced crystallized ginger
      (found in Oriental section of
      supermarket), divided

1. Dredge turkey in seasoned flour (shake off excess flour) and sauté in butter along with onions until lightly browned. Do not overcook.
2. Remove turkey to a plate and keep warm.
3. Add flour to skillet and stir over low heat about 3 minutes.
4. Blend in turkey stock, Madeira and cream. Stir until thickened.
5. Mix in 2 tablespoons crystallized ginger.
6. Pour sauce over turkey and garnish with remaining ginger.

This dish is very rich and is good served with chutney, curried rice, a crisp salad.

Orange Chutney Turkey

8 turkey cutlets
1 teaspoon salt
1/4 teaspoon pepper
2 tablespoons vegetable oil
1/2 cup orange juice
1 cup chutney, chopped
1/4 cup granulated sugar
2 tablespoons lemon juice
2 oranges, peeled and cut into
    1/2-inch slices
    (completely remove white membrane
    from around orange)
1 tablespoon cornstarch
2 tablespoons water

1. Sprinkle cutlets with salt and pepper and sauté in oil. Do not overcook.
2. Place cutlets in shallow baking pan (one that can later be heated on top of the stove).
3. Add orange juice, cover and bake 350 degrees for 25 minutes.
4. Combine chutney, sugar and lemon juice.
5. Place orange slices over turkey and pour chutney mixture over.
6. Continue baking, uncovered, for 15 additional minutes.
7. Remove turkey and orange slices to warm serving platter.
8. Place baking pan on stove and bring pan juices to a boil.
9. Combine cornstarch and water.
10. Lower heat, slowly add cornstarch mixture, and stir constantly until sauce thickens.
11. Pour sauce over turkey and serve.

Turkey, Cheese and Ham Puffs

Serves 4

8 turkey cutlets
2½ cups turkey stock
1/2 cup dry sherry
6 tablespoons prepared mustard
3/4 teaspoon garlic salt
3/4 teaspoon Fines Herbs
    (1/4 teaspoon each: sage,
    dry basil and thyme)
8 large slices Jack cheese (4x6)
8 large slices cooked ham (4x6)
1 package frozen patty shells, thawed
    30 minutes at room temperature
1 egg white, beaten
sesame seeds or poppy seeds (optional)

1. Early in the day, place cutlets, sherry and stock in large sauce pan. Bring to boil, reduce heat, cover and simmer 10 minutes or until tender.

2. Let cool 30 minutes in stock. Remove cutlets from stock and refrigerate until ready to use. (Reserve stock for Pat's gravy, see page 74)

3. Blend mustard, garlic salt and herbs and spread over each cutlet.

4. Wrap each cutlet with a slice of cheese, then a slice of ham.

5. On a lightly floured board, roll each patty shell into 8-inch circle.

6. Set cheese-and-ham-wrapped cutlet, seam side down, in center of pastry circle. Bring up sides to overlap and pinch to seal. Bring up ends and do the same.

7. Place puffs, seam side down, on large ungreased baking sheet at least 2 inches apart. Brush with egg white and sprinkle with seeds.

8. Chill 30 minutes (or longer) and then bake 425 degrees for 30 minutes until richly brown and crisp. Serve with Pat's gravy.

John's Turkey Parmesan

8 large turkey cutlets, pounded thin
1/2 cup flour
1/4 cup butter
1 large onion, chopped
3 cloves garlic, minced
1 tablespoon basil
1 teaspoon thyme
1 tablespoon oregano
1 tablespoon marjoram
1 can (29-ounce) tomato sauce
1/3 cup white wine
8 slices Mozzarella or Jack cheese
1 cup grated Parmesan cheese
parsley to garnish

1. Dredge the cutlets with flour and sauté them in butter until lightly browned. Do not overcook. Remove from pan.

2. In same pan, sauté onions and garlic with seasonings.

3. Add tomato sauce and wine and mix well.

4. Place 1/2 the sauce in bottom of shallow baking dish.

5. Place cutlets in baking dish in the sauce.

6. Place one slice of cheese on each cutlet (can be grated).

7. Cover with remaining sauce and sprinkle with Parmesan cheese and parsley.

8. Bake in 350 degree oven for 30 minutes.

Variations

1. Use cracker crumbs or bread crumbs in place of flour.

2. Two cans (15-ounce each) Pizza sauce can be used for the sauce instead of tomato sauce and seasonings.

3. Add sauteed mushrooms to the tomato sauce.

Turkey Cutlets with Rhubarb Dressing

Serves 4

8 turkey cutlets
1/3 cup flour
1/2 teaspoon crushed rosemary
3/4 teaspoon salt
1/8 teaspoon pepper
1/4 cup butter
4 slices firm-textured bread, cut into 1/2-inch cubes
2/3 cup firmly packed brown sugar
1/2 teaspoon cinnamon
1/4 teaspoon allspice
3 large stalks rhubarb, cut into 1/2-inch pieces
3 tablespoons flour
1/2 cup water

1. Dredge cutlets in flour and sprinkle with rosemary, salt and pepper.

2. Heat butter in skillet and sauté cutlets on both sides until lightly browned. Do not overcook. Reserve drippings.

3. In bowl, combine bread, sugar, cinnamon, allspice, rhubarb and flour. Spread one-half of bread mixture in greased, shallow baking dish.

4. Arrange cutlets on top of bread mixture and cover with remaining bread.

5. Combine drippings and water and pour over the top.

6. Cover and bake at 350 degrees for 45 minutes. Uncover and bake 15 additional minutes.

Baked Turkey, Mexican Style

This is a terrific dish for late summer when the tomatoes are at their best.

12 turkey cutlets
2 eggs, beaten
bottled taco sauce, divided
1/4 teaspoon salt
2 cups unflavored taco chips, crushed (or bread crumbs or cornmeal)
2 teaspoons chili powder
2 teaspoons ground cumin
1½ teaspoon garlic salt
1/2 teaspoon oregano
1/4 cup butter
4 cups shredded Iceberg lettuce
1 cup sour cream
1/3 cup chopped green onion (tops included)
1½ cups chopped fresh tomatoes
2 limes, cut into wedges
1 ripe avocado, peeled, pitted, sliced

1. In small dish, combine eggs, 4 to 5 tablespoons taco sauce and salt.

2. In another dish, combine taco chips, chili powder, cumin, garlic salt and oregano.

3. Dip each cutlet in egg mixture to coat and then in crumbs. Set aside.

4. Melt butter in shallow baking pan and place cutlets in pan, turning each cutlet to coat in butter.

5. Bake at 375 degrees for 35 minutes.

6. Serve on bed of lettuce and garnish with sour cream, green onion, tomatoes, lime wedges and avocado. Pass the taco sauce.

Turkey Cutlets with Brandy and Sherry

8 turkey cutlets
salt and pepper
1/2 teaspoon paprika
3 tablespoons vegetable oil
1 green onion, chopped
1/4 teaspoon marjoram
2 tablespoons chopped onion
2 tablespoons chopped parsley, divided
1 clove garlic, crushed
1/2 cup cream
3 tablespoons brandy
3 tablespoons sherry
2 egg yolks, well beaten

1. Heat oil on medium heat and sprinkle cutlets with salt, pepper and paprika. Sauté cutlets until golden brown on both sides. Do not overcook.

2. Add green onion, marjoram, onion, 1 tablespoon parsley, and garlic. Cover and simmer about 10 minutes. Add a little water if dry.

3. Remove cutlets to warm serving plate.

4. Combine cream, brandy, sherry and egg yolks. Stir into skillet and place over low heat.

5. Cook, stirring constantly, until thickened slightly and heated through.

6. Pour over cutlets and sprinkle with remainder of parsley.

Turkey Piccata

8 turkey cutlets, pounded thin
1/2 cup flour
1½ teaspoons salt
1/4 teaspoon pepper (freshly ground is best)
1 teaspoon paprika
1/4 cup butter
1 tablespoon olive oil
2 to 4 tablespoons dry Madeira
3 tablespoons fresh lemon juice (you could use bottled, but fresh is best)
lemon slices (buy 2 lemons, one for juice and one for slices)
3 to 4 tablespoons capers (optional)
1/4 cup minced fresh parsley

1. Combine flour, salt, pepper and paprika in a bag. Add the cutlets and coat well. Shake off excess flour mixture.

2. Sauté cutlets in combined butter and olive oil 2 to 3 minutes per side. Remove from heat.

3. Drain off all but 2 tablespoons butter mixture. Add Madeira and scrape bottom of skillet to loosen any browned bits.

4. Add lemon juice and heat briefly until sauce thickens (a matter of minutes).

5. Return cutlets to skillet, interspersing with lemon slices and heat briefly.

6. Place cutlets, lemon slices and sauce on serving dish. Garnish with capers and minced parsley and serve immediately.

This is a fabulous party dish which goes well with fettuccini and fresh broccoli.

Apple Stuffed Cutlets

8 to 10 turkey cutlets, pounded thin
salt and pepper to taste
1 cup soft bread crumbs, crusts removed
   (2 slices bread)
1/4 cup milk
2 tablespoons butter
1 large apple, peeled and diced
1 medium onion, diced
1/2 cup raisins
1/2 teaspoon sage
1 egg plus 2 tablespoons water, beaten
1½ cups cracker crumbs
Pat's gravy (see page 74)

1. Season cutlets with salt and pepper.

2. Soften bread crumbs with milk.

3. Heat butter in skillet and sauté apple and onion until tender crisp.

4. Add raisins and sage. Combine onion mixture with bread crumbs.

5. Place a small amount of filling in each cutlet and roll up. Secure with a toothpick if necessary.

6. Brush stuffed cutlet with egg mixture and roll in cracker crumbs.

7. Place in buttered shallow baking dish and bake, covered, at 350 degrees for 10 minutes. Uncover and bake 10 additional minutes. Add Pat's gravy and bake another 5 to 10 minutes.

This is a great fall meal served with squash or sweet potatoes.

Baked Turkey Italiana

This is a wonderful party dish as it serves so many and can be prepared in advance.

24 turkey cutlets
5 cups bread crumbs
2 cups fresh grated Parmesan cheese
1 tablespoon salt
1/3 cup chopped parsley
1½ cups butter
3 cloves garlic, crushed
1 tablespoon Dijon mustard
1 tablespoon Worcestershire sauce

1. In a large bowl, combine bread crumbs, cheese, salt, and parsley.
2. Melt butter in a large skillet and add garlic, mustard, and Worcestershire sauce. Mix well and cool slightly.
3. Dip the cutlets in the butter mixture and roll in the crumb-cheese mixture, coating each piece completely (Cutlets can be refrigerated here.).
4. Place cutlets in shallow baking pans in a single layer and bake 350 degrees for 45 minutes.

For a slight variation in flavor, add 1 tablespoon rosemary in place of the mustard and Worcestershire sauce.

Sweet and Sour Turkey

Serves 4

8 large turkey cutlets
2 eggs, beaten
1/2 cup flour
garlic salt to taste
2 tablespoons vegetable oil
1 tablespoon butter
1 can (20-ounce) pineapple chunks, drain and reserve juice
1/3 cup vinegar
1/4 cup dry sherry
3/4 cup ketchup
1 teaspoon monosodium glutamate
1 teaspoon soy sauce
1½ teaspoons salt

Ah-Soooo Good!

1. Dip turkey cutlets in egg and then in flour.
2. Sprinkle both sides with garlic salt.
3. Let sit for 30 minutes.
4. Sauté cutlets on both sides in oil and butter mixture until golden brown. Do not overcook. Arrange in shallow baking dish.
5. Heat pineapple juice and combine with remaining ingredients.
6. Add pineapple chunks to sauce.
7. Pour sauce over the turkey cutlets and bake, uncovered, at 350 degrees for 30 minutes.

This dish is very good served with rice and a green salad. The sauce can be spooned over the rice.

Heather's Beef and Turkey

Serves 6

12 turkey cutlets
1 jar (4-ounce) chipped or dried beef
12 bacon strips
1 cup sour cream
1 can (10¾-ounce) cream of mushroom
   soup
1 tablespoon flour

1. Line a shallow baking dish with the beef.
2. Roll each cutlet in a strip of bacon. Place on the beef in the baking dish.
3. Combine the sour cream, mushroom soup and flour. Pour over cutlets.
4. Bake, uncovered, 3 hours at 275 degrees.

Give it a try.... Pleeez?

Judy's Turkey a l'Orange

Serves 4

8 turkey cutlets
seasoned flour (1/2 cup flour, 1 teaspoon salt, 1/2 teaspoon paprika,
   1/4 teaspoon pepper)
2 tablespoons vegetable oil
1 tablespoon butter
2 tablespoons brown sugar
1/2 teaspoon ginger
1/4 cup flour
1½ cups orange juice
1½ cups water
1/2 teaspoon Tabasco® sauce
1 orange, peeled and cut into
   1/2-inch thick slices
6 small sweet potatoes, cooked
   and peeled

1. Dredge cutlets in seasoned flour.
2. Sauté cutlets in oil and butter mixture. Do not overcook. Remove and keep warm.
3. In same skillet, add brown sugar, ginger, flour, orange juice, water and Tabasco® sauce.
4. Heat and stir until smooth and thickened.
5. Add turkey and simmer until done (approximately 15 minutes).
6. Surround turkey with sliced orange and sweet potatoes.
7. Cover and heat through.

Turkey with Artichokes

8 to 10 turkey cutlets
1 cup flour
salt and pepper to taste
2 tablespoons vegetable oil
2 tablespoons butter
2 jars (6-ounce each) marinated artichoke hearts, drained
1/2 pound whole fresh mushrooms
1 can (6-ounce) pearl onions, drained (or small fresh boiling onions
**   which have been par-boiled)**
1/2 green pepper, chopped
2 cups white sauce (see page 75)
1/2 cup sherry,
1 teaspoon rosemary (or tarragon)
2 teaspoons paprika

1. Dredge cutlets in flour and season with salt and pepper.

2. Heat oil and butter in large skillet and sauté cutlets until golden brown. Do not overcook.

3. Place cutlets in large shallow baking dish and surround with artichokes, mushrooms, onions and peppers.

4. Prepare white sauce. Add sherry and rosemary and pour over ingredients in baking dish. Sprinkle with paprika.

5. Cover and bake 350 degrees for 45 minutes.

Add a sprinkle of Thompson seedless grapes the last 15 minutes of baking. It makes a really festive and pretty dish.

Fresh Tomato Cutlets

Serves 4

This is an especially good recipe to use when tomatoes are in season. Serve it with a freshly tossed salad and garden vegetables.

8 large turkey cutlets
2 tablespoons olive oil
1 medium onion, chopped
2 cloves garlic, minced
3 fresh tomatoes, peeled and chopped
1 bay leaf, crushed

1/2 teaspoon thyme
1 tablespoon basil (fresh is best)
salt and pepper to taste
1/4 cup vegetable oil
1 cup bread or cracker crumbs
1 teaspoon dry mustard

1. To prepare sauce, heat olive oil in large sauce pan and sauté onions and garlic until golden.

2. Add tomatoes, bay leaf, thyme, basil, salt and pepper to taste. Simmer ingredients.

3. While sauce simmers, heat oil in large skillet.

4. Toss cutlets in crumbs and sauté until golden. Do not overcook.

5. Sprinkle both sides with salt, pepper and mustard.

6. Mound tomato mixture over cutlets and simmer, covered, until cutlets are tender (about 15 minutes).

Variation

For a completely different flavor, make it Mexican style.

Sauté 2 stalks thinly sliced celery along with onions and garlic. Add 1 can (4-ounce) chopped green chiles, drained. In place of other seasonings, use 1/4 teaspoon ground cumin, 1/2 teaspoon oregano, and 1/2 teaspoon sugar. Before serving, top with 1½ cups shredded Cheddar cheese.

Turkey Scaloppine

Serves 4

8 large turkey cutlets, pounded thin
1/2 cup turkey stock
2 tablespoons vegetable oil
2 tablespoons butter
1/3 cup chopped onion
1/2 pound fresh mushrooms, sliced
1 clove garlic, minced
1/2 teaspoon salt
1/2 teaspoon marjoram
1/2 teaspoon thyme
2 tablespoons lemon juice
1 tablespoon cornstarch
1/2 cup Marsala wine (dry sherry is good, too)
2 tablespoons chopped parsley

1. Heat oil in skillet and sauté cutlets until golden. Do not overcook.

2. Place cutlets in shallow baking dish and keep warm.

3. Add butter to skillet and sauté onions until partially done. Add mushrooms and garlic and sauté until tender but do not overcook.

4. Add salt, herbs and lemon juice. Combine cornstarch, turkey stock, and wine and add to the onions and mushrooms, blending well until smooth.

5. Pour over cutlets and bake for 15 to 20 minutes at 350 degrees.

6. Garnish with parsley and serve immediately.

100

Main Dishes

Main Dishes, continued

Main Dishes, continued

Lynette's Turkey Tetrazzini

Serves 8

4 cups cooked turkey pieces
2¼ cups turkey stock
3 tablespoons olive oil, divided
1 medium onion, chopped
3 stalks celery, chopped
1 large red bell pepper, chopped
1 large green bell pepper, chopped
1/4 cup chopped parsley
3/4 pound fresh mushrooms, sliced
2 cloves garlic, minced
2 teaspoons oregano
2 teaspoons basil
1/2 teaspoon nutmeg

1 teaspoon salt
1/4 teaspoon pepper
1/2 cup dry sherry
1/4 cup half and half
2 egg yolks, beaten
2 tablespoons flour
3 tablespoons water
4 hard-cooked eggs, coarsely chopped
12 ounces linguini, cooked
   and drained
12 ounces Parmesan cheese, grated
12 ounces Provalone, thinly sliced
2 teaspoons paprika

1. In large skillet, heat 1 tablespoon olive oil and sauté onion, celery, and peppers.

2. In a large sauce pan, heat remaining oil and sauté parsley, mushrooms, garlic and spices. Add the onion mixture.

3. Add turkey stock, sherry, half and half, and egg yolks. Combine the flour and water to make a paste and add to sauce to thicken. Add turkey pieces and hard-cooked egg.

4. Combine 2 cups of the sauce with the cooked linguini.

5. Spread a thin layer of the sauce in the bottom of a shallow baking dish.

6. Add one-half of the linguini mixture.

7. Sprinkle with a layer of Parmesan cheese and add a layer of Provalone slices. Cover with half of the remaining sauce. Repeat layers.

8. Top with Parmesan cheese and paprika.

9. Bake at 350 degrees for 30 to 45 minutes.

Heather's Hawaiian Curry

6 cups cooked turkey pieces
3 tablespoons white wine vinegar
2 teaspoons salt
3 tablespoons chili powder
1½ tablespoons curry powder
1/2 green chili, chopped
2 cloves garlic, minced
1 (2-inch) cinnamon stick
1/4 teaspoon cardamom
2 whole cloves
2 teaspoons turmeric
3 tablespoons vegetable oil
2 bay leaves
1/2 teaspoon dill seed
5 cups coconut milk (usually found in the frozen section of Oriental stores)
juice of 1/2 of lime
hot cooked rice
condiments of your choice

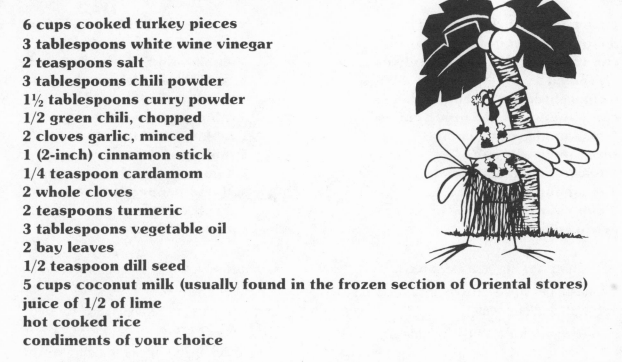

1. Mix all ingredients except lime, rice, and condiments together and cook slowly for 2 to 3 hours. The curry should thicken naturally.

2. Remove bay leaves and whole cloves.

3. Sprinkle with lime juice just before serving.

4. Serve over hot cooked rice with choice of condiments.

Suggested condiments are:

chopped peanuts	banana pieces
chutney	chopped egg (hard-cooked)
coconut	mandarin oranges, chopped
raisins	chopped dates
chopped green onion	pineapple tidbits

Turkey-Filled Acorn Squash

Serves 4

2 cups cooked turkey pieces
1/3 cup chopped green onion
1 can (2½-ounce) sliced ripe olives, drained
1½ cups shredded Cheddar cheese
1 can (4-ounce) diced green chiles
3/4 teaspoon ground cumin
1 teaspoon garlic salt
1/4 teaspoon paprika
1/4 teaspoon pepper
1/2 cup sour cream
2 acorn squash

1. Cut squash in half and remove seeds.
2. Turn squash, cavity side down, in shallow baking dish with 1/2 cup water.
3. Bake 350 degrees for about 45 minutes, or until tender.
4. Combine remaining ingredients together and mix well.
5. Remove squash from oven, salt and pepper to taste, and fill each cavity with equal amount of turkey mixture.
6. Return squash to oven and bake 20 minutes longer until well heated.

Madi's Geschnetzeltes

Serves 4

4 cups uncooked turkey breast, cut into small strips
1 small onion, finely chopped
1 cup sliced fresh mushrooms
1 clove garlic, minced
2 tablespoons olive oil
1 tablespoon butter
1 tablespoon flour
1/4 cup vermouth
salt and pepper to taste
1/2 cup cream
squeeze of lemon

1. Sauté onion, mushrooms and garlic in oil and butter mixture. Remove with slotted spoon.
2. Sauté meat in remaining oil for 3 to 4 minutes. Do not overcook.
3. Add onion, garlic and mushrooms to turkey in pan.
4. Sprinkle with flour, add vermouth and gently cook for a few minutes until all is well-heated.
5. Season to taste; add cream. Heat thoroughly but do not boil.
6. Just before serving, squeeze a lemon over all.

This is very nice served with buttered noodles garnished with chopped parsley.

Turkey Soufflé

This is a wonderful recipe for company because it's done the day ahead and is delicious. It's great for New Year's Eve supper.

2 cups cooked turkey pieces
12 slices white bread, cubed and crusts removed
1 cup chopped celery
1 onion, chopped
1 green pepper, chopped
1/4 pound fresh mushrooms, sliced
4 eggs, beaten
1 cup mayonnaise
3 cups milk
1 can (10¾-ounce) cream of mushroom soup (or cream of chicken)
1 cup grated Cheddar cheese

1. Put half of the cubed bread in buttered shallow baking dish.
2. Mix turkey, celery, onion, green pepper, and mushrooms together and put over bread.
3. Put remaining bread on top of turkey mixture.
4. Mix beaten eggs, mayonnaise, and milk together and pour over all.
5. Refrigerate overnight.
6. Before baking, spoon soup over top. Bake at 325 degrees for 45 minutes.
7. Top with cheese and paprika and bake 15 additional minutes.

Lynn's Enchiladas

4 cups cooked turkey pieces
1 package (8-ounce) softened cream cheese
2 tablespoons butter
1 medium onion, chopped
1 can (4-ounce) diced green
    chiles, drained

1/2 teaspoon pepper
8 flour tortillas
1½ cups grated Cheddar cheese
sour cream sauce (see below)

1. In large bowl, combine turkey pieces and cream cheese.

2. Sauté onions and chiles in butter. Combine with turkey mixture and add pepper.

3. Fill tortillas with turkey mixture, roll up and place seam side down in buttered shallow baking dish. Pour sauce over all and top with grated cheese.

4. Place in 350 degree oven and bake 30 minutes.

Slices of red bell pepper would make a colorful garnish.

Sour Cream Sauce

1 cup turkey stock
2 tablespoons butter
1/2 cup diced onion
1/4 cup diced green pepper
1/2 cup shredded carrot

1 clove garlic, minced
2 tablespoons flour
1 cup sour cream
1/2 teaspoon ground cumin
salt to taste

1. In large skillet, melt butter and sauté onion, green pepper, carrot, and garlic.

2. Stir in flour and cook one minute.

3. Add turkey stock and cook until mixture thickens.

4. Stir cumin into sour cream. Add a little hot stock mixture to the sour cream to heat and then stir back into the stock mixture.

5. Cook over low heat until heated thoroughly. Salt sauce to taste.

Turkey Turnovers with Corn Chip Crust

Serves 4

1¼ cups cooked turkey pieces, very finely chopped
1 package (3-ounce) cream cheese, softened
1 tablespoon milk
1 cup shredded Cheddar cheese
1 can (4-ounce) chopped green chiles
1/4 cup sliced green onions
1/2 teaspoon garlic powder
1/2 teaspoon salt
1/2 teaspoon ground cumin
2 cups buttermilk baking mix
1/2 cup water
3 tablespoons melted butter
1-1/3 cups crushed corn chips

1. Mix softened cream cheese with milk. Add turkey, cheese, chiles, onion and seasonings. Set aside.

2. Stir baking mix with water until blended and turn onto floured board. Knead about 10 times to form a ball.

3. Roll out a 12 by 18-inch rectangle and cut into 6-inch squares.

4. Spoon 1/3 cup turkey mixture onto each square. Fold squares corner to corner to form triangles and press edges with a fork to seal.

5. Brush stuffed triangles with melted butter and then press turnovers into crushed chips to coat.

6. Place on ungreased cookie sheet and bake 400 degrees for 20 minutes.

Leslie's Quick Casserole

Serves 4

2 cups cooked turkey pieces
2 cups cooked noodles (rotini noodles are excellent)
2 cups uncooked broccoli flowers
1/2 cup mayonnaise
1/2 cup sour cream
1 can (10¾-ounce) cream of chicken soup
1 tablespoon lemon juice
1½ cups grated Swiss cheese

1. Combine turkey, noodles, and broccoli.
2. Combine remaining ingredients, except save 1/2 cup cheese for garnish.
3. Add to turkey mixture and place in buttered casserole.
4. Bake 350 degrees for 30 minutes. Add remaining cheese and bake an additional 5 minutes.

You can make 1½ cups Velouté Sauce (see page 75) in place of the canned soup.

Be still, my heart.

Chinese-Style Goulash

Serves 6

2 cups cooked turkey pieces
2 cups turkey stock
1/4 cup butter
1 small onion, sliced
1 cup fresh sliced mushrooms
1 cup uncooked regular rice
1 green pepper, cut into thin strips
1/2 cup chopped celery
1/4 cup half and half
salt and pepper to taste

1. Melt butter in large skillet.
2. Sauté onion and mushrooms in butter until tender crisp.
3. Add stock and heat to boiling.
4. Stir in rice.
5. Reduce heat, cover and simmer for 20 minutes.
6. Stir in remaining ingredients.
7. Cover and cook 10 minutes longer.

Ah-Soooo Good!

Janie's Turkey Divan

Serves 8

This recipe works wonderfully well using asparagus instead of broccoli. Try it both ways.

2 cups cooked turkey pieces
2 packages (10-ounce each) frozen
broccoli (or 2 to 3 pounds fresh)
2 cans (10¾-ounce each) cream of
chicken soup (or celery soup)
1 cup mayonnaise
1 teaspoon lemon juice
1/2 teaspoon curry (or more,
to taste)
1 cup grated sharp Cheddar cheese
(Swiss cheese is also good)
1/2 cup soft bread crumbs
1 tablespoon melted butter

1. Cook and drain broccoli.

2. Arrange broccoli in buttered shallow baking dish.

3. Place turkey over broccoli.

4. Combine soup, mayonnaise, lemon juice and curry powder. Pour over turkey.

5. Sprinkle cheese over top.

6. Combine bread crumbs and butter and sprinkle over cheese.

7. Bake in pre-heated 350 degree oven for 30 minutes.

You can make 1½ cups Velouté Sauce (see page 75) instead of the canned soup. This would also be a great way to use left-over gravy.

Sue's Turkey-Wild Rice

Serves 6

3 cups cooked turkey pieces
1 box Uncle Ben's® long grain
and wild rice
2 cans (10¾-ounce each) cream of
celery soup
1/2 cup mayonnaise
1 package (10-ounce) frozen
green peas, (optional)
1/2 cup chopped onions
1 small jar chopped pimientos
1/2 cup slivered almonds
1 cup grated Swiss cheese
(Cheddar is also good)

1. Prepare rice according to directions on box.

2. Combine all ingredients except cheese; place in shallow baking dish.

3. Bake at 350 degrees for 30 minutes.

4. Top with cheese and return to oven for additional 10 minutes.

Experiment!

111

Almond Turkey in a Crust

3 cups cooked turkey pieces
1 cup shredded Cheddar cheese
1 tablespoon flour
1 cup blanched slivered almonds, divided
1½ cups sliced celery
1 tablespoon lemon juice
1 cup mayonnaise
1/2 teaspoon poultry seasoning
1/2 teaspoon salt
1/8 teaspoon pepper
pastry for a 2 crust 9-inch pie (see page 182)
lemon wedges and parsley for garnish

1. Toss the cheese in the flour.
2. Combine 3/4 cup cheese and flour mixture, 1/2 cup almonds, and all remaining ingredients except pastry. Mix well.
3. Roll pastry into large rectangle. Fit into a 9x13 baking dish and trim to 1 inch beyond edge. Flute edge.
4. Fill with turkey mixture.
5. Top with remaining cheese and flour mixture and remaining almonds.
6. Bake 400 degrees for 30 to 35 minutes.
7. Garnish with lemon wedges and parsley, if desired.

This is best served with the pastry but is delicious even without. Try it both ways.

Artichokes in Rice-Spinach Pieshell

Serves 4

1½ cups cooked turkey pieces
1 package (10-ounce) frozen
  chopped spinach
2 cups cooked white or brown rice
4 tablespoons soft butter, divided
1 package (9-ounce) artichoke hearts,
  thawed
1 cup shredded Swiss cheese
1/4 pound fresh mushrooms, sliced
2 tablespoons flour
1/2 teaspoon curry powder
1/2 teaspoon garlic powder
1 teaspoon prepared mustard
1 cup milk
salt and pepper to taste

trust me!

1. Cook spinach and drain well, squeezing out all liquid.

2. Combine spinach, rice and 2 tablespoons butter. Press into well-greased 9-inch pie pan. Cover and chill about 1 hour.

3. Blot artichokes dry, then cut each into 2 or 3 pieces.

4. Arrange artichokes over rice crust, top with turkey, then with cheese.

5. Melt remaining 2 tablespoons butter in frying pan and sauté mushrooms until golden.

6. Stir in flour and curry powder and cook until bubbly.

7. Add garlic powder and mustard and gradually stir in milk. Cook and stir until thickened. Season with salt and pepper to taste.

8. Pour sauce over pie. (It can be covered and chilled at this point.)

9. Bake uncovered at 350 degrees for 45 minutes to 1 hour.

This is delicious served with spiced fruit.

Quesadeas

Serves 6

2 cups cooked turkey pieces, finely chopped
2 cups shredded Jack cheese
1 can (4-ounce) diced green chiles, drained
1 cup chopped green onion
6 flour tortillas (large size used for burritos)
1/2 cup vegetable oil

1. In center of each tortilla, arrange the first four ingredients in layers.
2. Fold all sides toward the center so filling cannot fall out.
3. In fry pan, heat oil over medium high and sauté quesadeas, seam side down, until golden. Turn and sauté other side.

This is a meal in itself and is wonderful served with a green salad. Make plenty of quesadeas because they are delicious reheated in the microwave the next day.

Variations

1. Cheddar or Swiss cheese are also excellent choices.
2. Try adding chopped tomatoes, ripe olives, mushrooms and/or shredded iceberg lettuce for a super deluxe quesadea.
3. Add cooked chopped bacon.
4. Add taco sauce to the filling.
5. Pass the salsa with the cooked quesadeas.
6. Use corn crepes in place of tortillas (see page 138)
7. Instead of frying, bake at 350 degrees for 20 to 30 minutes.

Mexican Turkey with Green Sauce

Serves 10

6 cups large cooked turkey pieces
green sauce (see below)
1 pint sour cream
1 dozen 6-inch corn or flour tortillas, cut into 2-inch pieces
1½ pounds Jack cheese, shredded

1. Arrange half the turkey pieces in a lightly greased 9x13 baking dish.

2. Cover with half the green sauce and half the sour cream.

3. Top with half the tortilla pieces and half the cheese.

4. Repeat layers exactly the same. (Can be refrigerated if desired.)

5. Bake, covered, at 375 degrees for 40 minutes.

6. Uncover and bake an additional 8 minutes or until cheese is bubbly.

7. Cut into squares to serve.

Green Sauce

1 can (14-ounce) Mexican tomatillos, drained
1 small onion, cut into pieces
2 cloves garlic
1 can (4-ounce) chopped green chiles
1 bunch (about 1/2 cup) chopped fresh cilantro (also called coriander or Chinese parsley)
1 teaspoon salt
1/2 teaspoon sugar

Combine all ingredients into a blender and whirl until smoothly pureed.

Turkey Almond-Noodles

Serves 6

2 cups cooked turkey pieces
3/4 cup mayonnaise
1/3 cup flour
2 tablespoons minced onion (instant)
1 teaspoon garlic salt
2¼ cups milk
1 cup shredded Swiss or Jack cheese
1/3 cup dry white wine
7 ounces spaghetti, cooked and drained
1 package (10-ounce) frozen chopped
**   broccoli, thawed and drained**
1¼ cups sliced almonds, divided
1 cup sliced fresh mushrooms
1/4 cup chopped pimiento

1. In sauce pan, combine mayonnaise, flour and seasonings.

2. Gradually add milk, cooking over low heat and stirring constantly until thickened.

3. Add cheese and wine. Stir until cheese melts.

4. In large bowl, combine cheese sauce with remaining ingredients, except 1/2 cup almonds. Toss lightly.

5. Pour mixture into baking dish. Top with remaining almonds.

6. Bake 350 degrees for 40 minutes.

Cousin Tony's Turkey Loaf

Serves 4

1 to 2 pounds ground turkey
2/3 cup uncooked oatmeal
1 large green pepper, diced
1/2 cup chopped onion
1 or 2 eggs (depending on moistness
**   desired), slightly beaten**
1/8 cup ketchup
6 tablespoons Worcestershire sauce
garlic salt to taste
**   (2 or more teaspoons)**

1. Mix all ingredients in a bowl. (Use your hands for best results.)

2. Place mixture in greased loaf pan and spread evenly.

3. Spread Tony's Sauce evenly over top of meat loaf.

4. Bake 350 degrees for 50 to 60 minutes.

Tony's Sauce

1/2 cup ketchup
1/4 cup Worcestershire sauce
1/2 to 1 teaspoon ground black pepper
(depending on taste)

1. Mix all ingredients together until sauce is consistency of heavy cream.

2. Pour over top of loaf and spread evenly.

Mushroom Quick Dinner

Serves 4

**1 cup cooked turkey pieces
(hindquarter is fine)**
**1 can (10¾-ounce) condensed cream
of celery soup**
**1 can (4-ounce) mushroom stems and
pieces (drained)**
1 tablespoon chopped pimiento
1 teaspoon parsley flakes
salt and pepper to taste
**1 package (12-ounce) chow
mein noodles**

1. Heat soup.
2. Stir in remaining ingredients except chow mein noodles.
3. Heat thoroughly.
4. Serve over chow mein noodles.

Easy Spanish Rice

Serves 6

2 cups cooked turkey pieces
2 cups instant rice, uncooked
1/2 cup sliced pimiento-stuffed olives
**2 cans (16-ounce each) stewed
tomatoes**
1/2 teaspoon crushed basil
1/4 teaspoon garlic powder
1/8 teaspoon pepper
1/2 cup shredded Cheddar cheese

1. Combine all ingredients except cheese.
2. Pour mixture into greased baking dish.
3. Bake at 350 degrees for 30 minutes, covered.
4. Uncover, top with cheese, and bake an additional 10 minutes.

Sherried Artichoke Turkey

Serves 8

6 cups large cooked turkey pieces
1½ cups turkey stock
1/2 cup butter
1/2 pound fresh mushrooms, sliced
1/3 cup finely chopped green onions
1/4 cup flour
1/2 cup sherry
1 teaspoon rosemary
2 cans (8½-ounce each) artichoke
hearts, drained and cut
into pieces

1. Heat butter in skillet and sauté mushrooms and onions until tender-crisp.

2. Sprinkle flour over mushrooms and onions and stir in stock, sherry and rosemary. Cook, stirring constantly, until sauce begins to thicken.

3. Arrange turkey and artichoke pieces in large buttered casserole.

4. Pour sauce over turkey and bake 350 degrees for 40 minutes.

Edwina's Broccoli-Cheese

Serves 6

2 cups cooked turkey pieces,
finely chopped
2 tablespoons butter
3 stalks celery, chopped
1 medium onion, chopped
1 package (10-ounce) chopped
broccoli, cooked and drained
1 can (10¾-ounce) cream of
mushroom soup
1 roll garlic cheese
Worcestershire sauce to taste
(about 4 shakes)
Tabasco® sauce to taste
(about 4 shakes)
2 cups cooked rice

1. Melt butter in skillet and sauté celery and onion until tender.

2. Add broccoli, soup, garlic cheese, Worcestershire sauce, Tabasco® sauce, turkey, and rice.

3. Place in buttered casserole and bake 350 degrees for 30 minutes.

To make a delicious dip, omit the rice and serve in a chafing dish with specialty crackers.

Lumpia (Egg Rolls)

Serves 4

2 cups cooked turkey pieces
2 tablespoons peanut oil
1 clove garlic, minced
3 to 4 green onions, chopped
1 bunch spinach leaves, cleaned
   and chopped
1 tablespoon sesame oil
salt and pepper to taste
2 tablespoons soy sauce
1 package egg roll skins
additional peanut oil (for deep
   fat frying)

1. In large skillet or wok, heat 2 tablespoons peanut oil and sauté garlic, onions and spinach leaves.

2. Season with sesame oil, spices, and soy sauce.

3. Add turkey. Cool enough to handle.

4. Wrap turkey mixture in skins and deep fry in hot peanut oil, seam side down.

5. Serve with extra soy sauce.

Easy Mexicali Casserole

Serves 4

4 cups cooked turkey pieces
   (hindquarter is fine)
1 cup turkey stock
1/4 cup butter
1 medium onion, diced
1/4 cup flour
1 jar (2-ounce) diced pimiento
1 can (2½-ounce) sliced
   black olives
1 can (4-ounce) diced green chiles
salt and pepper to taste
2 cups grated Jack cheese, divided

1. Melt butter in large fry pan.

2. Sauté onion until tender.

3. Add flour, stirring into butter mixture.

4. Add stock; cook until thickened and bubbly.

5. Mix in remaining ingredients, except for 1/2 cup cheese.

6. Spoon into buttered casserole and bake 350 degrees for 20 minutes.

7. Top with remaining cheese and bake an additional 10 minutes.

Serve with warmed tortillas.

Turkey Stroganoff

Serves 6

3 cups cooked turkey pieces
1/4 cup butter
3 cups coarsely chopped celery
2 cups coarsely chopped onions
1/2 teaspoon salt
1 teaspoon oregano
1/8 teaspoon pepper
1/4 teaspoon rosemary
1/4 teaspoon thyme
2 tablespoons flour
2 cups sour cream
chopped parsley for garnish
hot, cooked noodles

1. In large skillet, melt butter and add celery, onion, and seasonings. Cook until tender (about 15 minutes.

2. Add turkey.

3. Stir flour into sour cream and blend into turkey mixture.

4. Heat thoroughly. Garnish with parsley and serve over noodles.

Turkey-Corn Casserole

Serves 8

4 cups cooked turkey pieces
2 tablespoons vegetable oil
1 large onion, chopped
1 red bell pepper, seeded and diced
1/2 pound fresh mushrooms, sliced
1 tablespoon chili powder
2 cans (1 pound each) cream-style corn
1 can (8-ounce) tomato sauce
1 package (8-ounce) egg noodles,
cooked and drained
1 cup grated Parmesan cheese
chopped parsley for garnish

1. Heat oil in skillet and sauté onion, red pepper, mushrooms and chili powder.

2. In shallow casserole, combine cooked onion mixture, corn, tomato sauce, noodles and turkey. Mix thoroughly.

3. Sprinkle with Parmesan cheese. (Can be covered and chilled at this point).

4. Bake 350 degrees for 35 to 40 minutes.

5. Garnish with parsley before serving.

Connie's Turghetti

Serves 4

2 cups cooked turkey pieces
1/2 cup turkey stock
1¼ cups cooked spaghetti
1/4 cup chopped green pepper
1 small onion, chopped
1 can (10¾-ounce) cream of
    mushroom soup
1¾ cups grated Cheddar cheese
1/2 teaspoon salt
1/8 teaspoon pepper
1/4 cup pimiento

Combine all ingredients and bake at 350 degrees for 45 minutes.

Easy Turkey Pilaf

Serves 6

2 cups cooked turkey pieces
1 can (10¾-ounce) condensed
    cream of mushroom soup
1¼ cups hot water
1/4 cup dry sherry
2 tablespoons chopped pimiento
1½ cups dry, instant rice
1/2 packet (1/4 cup) dry onion soup mix

1. Combine soup and water in 2-quart casserole.
2. Stir in remaining ingredients.
3. Bake, covered, at 350 degrees for 1 hour.

Jan's Cold Turkey Pie

Serves 6

1½ cups cooked turkey pieces
1 cup pineapple tidbits, drained
1 cup chopped walnuts
1/2 cup chopped celery
1/2 cup chopped black olives, divided
1/2 cup shredded Cheddar cheese,
    divided
1 9-inch baked pie shell (see page 182)

Dressing

1 cup sour cream
2/3 cup mayonnaise

1. Mix sour cream and mayonnaise together as dressing.
2. Mix turkey, pineapple, walnuts, celery, 1/3 cup olives and 1/3 cup cheese together with 2/3 cup dressing.
3. Pour into baked pie shell.
4. Top with thin coating of remaining dressing.
5. Garnish with remainder of grated cheese and chopped olives.
6. Refrigerate for several hours and serve cold.

Turkey a la King

3 cups cooked turkey pieces
1/4 cup chopped green pepper
1/4 cup chopped onion
1 cup fresh mushrooms, thinly sliced
1/4 cup butter, divided
2 tablespoons flour
1/2 teaspoon salt
2 cups half and half
  (milk is good)
1 tablespoon lemon juice
3 tablespoons cooking sherry·
1/4 cup diced pimiento
3 egg yolks, beaten
1/2 teaspoon paprika
1/4 cup milk

1. In a small skillet sauté green pepper, onion and mushrooms in 2 tablespoons butter until tender crisp.

2. In a large sauce pan, melt remaining butter. Blend in flour and salt and gradually stir in half and half. Cook until sauce thickens but do not boil.

3. Add turkey, vegetables, lemon juice, sherry, and pimiento. Stir constantly to prevent lumps forming.

4. Blend egg yolks, paprika and milk. Add some of the heated sauce to warm and then stir back into sauce pan. Cook for three minutes or until mixture thickens slightly.

5. Remove from heat and serve over buttered toast.

Variations

1. Serve over baked puffed pastry shells, baking powder biscuits or toasted English muffins.

2. Add 1 cup frozen peas for a heartier meal.

3. Top with toasted almonds (bake 325 degrees for 10 minutes).

Turkey Lasagne

4 cups cooked turkey pieces (very finely chopped)
1/3 cup butter
1/2 pound fresh mushrooms, sliced
1/2 cup sauterne wine
10 ounces lasagne noodles
1/4 cup butter
1/4 cup flour
4 cups half and half
1/4 teaspoon tarragon
salt and pepper to taste
4 cups Jack cheese
1/4 cup grated Parmesan cheese
1/4 cup chopped parsley

1. Melt butter and sauté mushrooms until limp but not browned. Add wine and simmer until most of the wine evaporates.

2. Cook noodles according to package directions. Rinse and drain.

3. In sauce pan, melt butter and blend in flour. Slowly add half and half. (It is important to add slowly to keep sauce from curdling.) Cook until thickened but do not boil.

4. Add mushrooms and spices.

5. In a buttered shallow baking dish, alternate layers of noodles, turkey, sauce, and Jack cheese. Repeat three times.

6. Top with Parmesan cheese and parsley.

7. Bake at 350 degrees for 30 to 40 minutes. Let it rest for 10 minutes before serving.

Chalupas

3 cups cooked turkey pieces
2 tablespoons vegetable oil
1 medium onion, chopped
1 can (8-ounce) tomato sauce
1 bottle (7-ounce) taco sauce, divided
1 can (16-ounce) refried beans
1 large clove garlic, minced or pressed
1 cup shredded Cheddar cheese

condiments:

shredded iceberg lettuce
1 cup sour cream
chopped green onions
chopped ripe olives
chopped fresh cilantro
guacamole

1. Prepare fried cakes (see below)

2. Sauté onion in oil until golden brown. Add tomato sauce and 1/4 cup taco sauce, and simmer 5 minutes, stirring often.

3. Remove from heat. Add turkey pieces and place in covered casserole (2 quart).

4. Combine refried beans, garlic, 2 tablespoons taco sauce, and cheese. Place in shallow baking dish.

5. Bake both turkey (covered) and bean casserole (uncovered) at 350 degrees for 30 minutes. Stir beans often.

6. To assemble chalupas, spread fried cakes with guacamole, add a layer of bean casserole and a layer of turkey mixture. Serve with condiments.

Fried Cakes

1/4 cup softened butter
1½ cup masa harina (dehydrated masa flour)

1/2 teaspoon salt
3/4 cup water

1. Beat butter with electric beater until fluffy. Mix in flour, salt and water, beating until dough holds together (you might need a little more water or flour).

2. Divide dough into 5 equal parts and pat each one out on wax paper to a 5-inch circle. (This can be done the day ahead and refrigerated. Stack with waxed paper in between each one.)

3. Fry both sides on ungreased griddle until golden (about 3 minutes).

4. Stack, wrap in foil, and keep warm. (You can create a bowl effect by lining a bowl with the fried cake and letting it harden slightly.)

Try making the fried cakes, but if time is limited, you can substitute with corn or flour tortillas from the grocery store.

Joanne's Turkey Enchilada Casserole

Serves 10

6 cups large cooked turkey pieces
2 cans (10¾-ounce each) cream of mushroom soup
2 cans (10¾-ounce each) cream of chicken soup
2 large onions, chopped
1½ cans (4-ounce) diced green chiles, drained
2 cans (2½-ounce each) sliced ripe olives, drained
3/4 teaspoon cumin
1/4 teaspoon oregano
1 package corn or flour tortillas, torn into eighths
2½ pounds Jack cheese, grated
1½ pints sour cream, divided

1. Heat undiluted soup. Add onions, chiles, olives and seasonings.

2. Cover bottom of large casserole (or two 9x13) with layer of torn tortillas, then layer of turkey, then soup mixture, and then cheese.

3. Repeat layers until casserole is full, except in the middle layer put 1½ cups sour cream over cheese.

4. Cover and bake 325 degrees for 1 hour. (Bake less time if using two baking dishes.)

5. Uncover, add remaining sour cream, and bake 20 additional minutes.

In place of tortillas, try using the plain tortilla chips.

Aye yi-yi-yi!

Turkey Enchiladas with Sour Cream

Serves 6

3 cups cooked turkey pieces
2 cans (4-ounce each) chopped green chiles, drained
2 cups chopped onions
1 large clove garlic, minced
2 tablespoons olive oil (or vegetable oil)
1½ pounds fresh, ripe tomatoes, peeled and chopped
2 teaspoons salt, divided
1/2 teaspoon oregano
1/2 cup water
2 cups sour cream
2½ cups shredded Cheddar cheese, divided
1/3 cup vegetable oil
12 corn or flour tortillas

Aye yi-yi-yi!

1. Sauté chiles, onions, and garlic in olive oil.

2. Add tomatoes, 1 teaspoon salt, oregano, and water.

3. Simmer slowly, uncovered, until thick (about 30 minutes). Set aside.

4. Combine turkey, sour cream, 2 cups cheese, and remaining salt (1 teaspoon).

5. Heat vegetable oil and sauté tortillas quickly on each side. Drain on a paper towel.

6. Fill tortillas with turkey mixture, roll up, and arrange in large shallow baking dish, seam side down.

7. Pour chile sauce over the top and bake 350 degrees for 20 minutes.

8. Add remaining cheese and bake 5 minutes longer.

This is very spicy because of the green chiles. If you want it less spicy, use only half as many chiles.

Turkey Carioca

4 cups uncooked turkey pieces
1½ cups turkey stock
2 tablespoons vegetable oil
1 medium onion, chopped
12 green onions, chopped
2 tablespoons chopped parsley
1/8 teaspoon thyme
2 cups sliced fresh mushrooms
1 cup sauterne
salt and pepper to taste
1/4 cup flour
1/4 cup water
1 tablespoon sherry
1 tablespoon rum
1 tablespoon lemon juice

1. Quickly brown turkey pieces in oil. Do not overcook.
2. Place in large casserole (one that can be put on stove top) with onions, parsley, thyme, mushrooms, stock, sauterne and seasonings.
3. Bake, covered, for 45 minutes at 350 degrees.
4. Combine flour and water into a smooth paste. Add some hot gravy to the flour to heat and slowly stir back into gravy. Place casserole on top of stove and heat and stir to thicken gravy.
5. Add sherry, rum and lemon juice to gravy.

This is especially good served along with wild rice.

Harriet's Stir-Fry

Serves 4

2 cups uncooked turkey pieces
1/2 cup turkey stock
2 tablespoons soy sauce
1/4 teaspoon cayenne pepper
2 tablespoons cornstarch
2 tablespoons water
2 tablespoons vegetable oil

4 green onions, chopped
1 green pepper, cut into 1/2-inch strips
1/4 pound small fresh mushrooms
1 package (10-ounce) frozen Chinese pea pods
   (1/2 pound fresh)
1/2 pint cherry tomatoes, cut in half
hot cooked rice

1. In medium bowl, combine turkey, soy sauce and cayenne pepper.

2. In small cup, combine cornstarch and water.

3. Heat oil in skillet or wok, add turkey and cook and stir quickly until golden brown. Do not overcook. Remove turkey to a platter.

4. Add green onions, green pepper, and mushrooms to skillet and sauté until tender-crisp.

5. Combine stock and cornstarch mixture and add to skillet, stirring until sauce thickens and bubbles.

6. Add pea pods, tomatoes and turkey. Heat thoroughly.

7. Serve with rice.

Variations

1. Don't be limited to the vegetables in the recipe. Broccoli, carrots, celery, green beans, cauliflower, and zucchini are great. Just use your imagination.

2. Add 1 can (8-ounce) water chestnuts, drained and sliced, and 1 can (6-ounce) bamboo shoots, drained, and heat thoroughly.

3. Add 1 can (16-ounce) bean sprouts, drained.

4. Serve over chow mein noodles instead of rice.

Sweet and Pungent Turkey

Serves 6

3 cups uncooked turkey pieces,
    cut into chunks
2 eggs, beaten
1 cup flour
1/4 cup water
1/2 teaspoon salt
vegetable oil for deep frying
1 can (20-ounce) pineapple chunks,
    drained (reserve juice)
pepper to taste
3/4 cup brown sugar
1 cup vinegar
3 tablespoons molasses
1 large green pepper, cut into strips
3 tomatoes, peeled and diced
1 teaspoon salt
3 tablespoons cornstarch
1/4 cup water
hot cooked rice

Ah-Soooo Good!

1. Combine eggs with flour, water and salt. Add turkey and stir until coated.

2. Fry turkey in 2″ hot oil (375 degrees) for 5 minutes. Set aside.

3. In large sauce pan combine pineapple, pepper, brown sugar, vinegar, molasses, and green pepper.

4. Add enough water to the pineapple juice to make 1½ cups.

5. Add to pineapple mixture and bring to a boil, stirring constantly.

6. Add tomatoes and salt and simmer for 5 minutes.

7. Combine cornstarch with 1/4 cup water and stir into above mixture.

8. Cook until thickened, stirring constantly.

9. Add turkey and simmer 15 minutes. Serve over rice.

Turkey Fondue

4 cups uncooked chunks of turkey breast
2 cups turkey stock
2 tablespoons dry sherry
1/4 cup butter (optional)
Sour Cream Sauce (see below)
Sesame Curry Mayonnaise (see below)
Spicy Ketchup (see below)

1. Heat stock, sherry, and butter in fondue pot.
2. Cook individual chunks of turkey as desired and serve with sauces.

Sour Cream Sauce

1/2 cup sour cream
2 tablespoons crumbled Blue cheese
1/4 teaspoon salt
1/8 teaspoon onion powder
1½ teaspoons chopped parsley
dash of pepper
1 to 2 drops Tabasco® sauce

Mix all ingredients together and chill well before serving.

Sesame Curry Mayonnaise

1/2 cup mayonnaise
1½ teaspoon chopped onion
1½ teaspoon chopped green pepper
1/4 teaspoon curry powder
1½ teaspoon sesame seeds

Mix all ingredients together and chill well before serving.

Spicy Ketchup

1/2 cup ketchup
1 teaspoon prepared mustard
1 teaspoon tarragon wine vinegar
1/8 teaspoon dill weed

Mix all ingredients together. Chill before serving.

Lemon Turkey

Serves 25

This is a good informal party recipe because it serves so many.

10 cups uncooked small pieces turkey breast
2 cups turkey stock
1 cup peanut oil, divided
2 tablespoons cornstarch
2 tablespoons salt
1/4 cup finely grated lemon peel
1½ pounds snow peas, strings removed
1½ cups fresh sliced mushrooms
1/4 cup fresh lemon juice
3 tablespoons cornstarch
3 tablespoons cold water
1/2 teaspoon white pepper
salt to taste
hot cooked rice

1. Combine turkey, 1/4 cup oil, and 2 tablespoons cornstarch in large bowl and blend.

2. Heat remaining oil and salt in large skillet over medium high heat. Add turkey and sauté until it just turns white. Do not brown.

3. Sprinkle with lemon peel, add stock, peas and mushrooms and cook one minute.

4. Combine remaining ingredients, except rice, and pour over turkey. Continue cooking, stirring constantly until sauce thickens.

5. Adjust seasoning and serve immediately with rice.

Scott's Chinese Turkey

4 cups uncooked turkey pieces
1/2 cup flour
1 teaspoon salt
1/2 teaspoon paprika
1/4 teaspoon pepper
1/4 cup vegetable oil
1 tablespoon butter
1 cup diced celery
1/2 cup chopped green onions
1/2 cup chopped green pepper
3/4 cup milk
1 can (10¾-ounce) cream of chicken soup
chow mein noodles
slivered almonds

1. Coat turkey pieces with combination of flour, salt, paprika and pepper.

2. Brown in oil and butter mixture. Do not overcook. Remove to covered baking dish.

3. In same skillet, sauté celery, onions and green pepper.

4. Combine milk and soup and add to onion mixture.

5. Pour over turkey and bake at 350 degrees for 20 minutes, covered.

6. Combine chow mein noodles and almonds and place on top of turkey mixture.

7. Bake uncovered an additional 10 minutes.

You can make 1½ cups Velouté sauce (see page 75) instead of the canned soup.

Ah- Soooo Good!

Turkey and Apple Deep Dish Pie

Serves 10

3 cups uncooked turkey pieces
3/4 cup richer-flavored turkey stock,
    divided
1/2 cup flour
1/4 cup vegetable oil
4 cups sliced onions
2 tablespoons white wine vinegar
salt and pepper to taste

1/2 teaspoon ginger
1/2 teaspoon allspice
2 Granny Smith or Newton apples,
    unpeeled, cored, and thinly sliced
1 egg, beaten
pastry for 2 crust 9-inch pie
    (see page 182)

1. Lightly toss turkey in flour and sauté until crusty and browned. Do not overcook. Salt and pepper to taste. Remove with slotted spoon.

2. Add onion to skillet and sauté until softened.

3. Stir in 1/2 cup stock and bring to boil, scraping all browned bits off surface of skillet. Reduce sauce to thick glaze.

4. Remove from heat, stir in vinegar and season to taste with salt and pepper.

5. Generously grease 9-inch springform pan.

6. Roll out 3/4 of pastry to fit pan, leaving 1/2-inch overhang. Chill in refrigerator for 20 minutes.

7. Layer 1/2 of turkey in bottom of pan and sprinkle with ginger and allspice. Arrange 1/2 of apples over turkey and top with 1/2 of onion mixture. Repeat layering.

8. Trim remaining pastry to fit top of pie and crimp top and bottom pastries together.

9. Cut hole in center of top and brush pastry with egg. Pour reduced stock through hole.

10. Set pan on baking sheet and bake 25 minutes 375 degrees.

11. Reduce oven to 350 degrees and bake an additional hour.

12. Let stand in pan about 10 minutes before unmolding. Slice into wedges and serve hot.

This is good with a layer of 1/2 cup raisins added to the turkey, apple and onion.

For a smaller and simpler version, reduce the amounts and bake in a 9-inch pie pan and do not unmold before serving.

133

Turkey Pilaf

Serves 6

3 cups uncooked turkey pieces
    (white meat is best)
2½ cups turkey stock, seasoned with:
    1/2 teaspoon oregano
    1/2 teaspoon basil
    1/2 teaspoon thyme
    1/2 teaspoon marjoram
    1/2 teaspoon parsley

3 garlic cloves, minced
1 cup chopped onion
2 tablespoons vegetable oil
2 tablespoons butter
1 cup rice or bulgar wheat
1 teaspoon garlic salt
1/2 cup raisins
2 tablespoons butter

1. Season stock and simmer.
2. In large skillet, sauté turkey, garlic and onion in combination of oil and butter until barely done. Do not overcook.
3. Remove turkey mixture from skillet and set aside.
4. Into same pan, add rice, garlic salt and stock. Cover.
5. Reduce heat and cook for 20 minutes.
6. Add turkey mixture, cover and cook 5 minutes longer.
7. Quickly sauté raisins in butter and add to pilaf.

Variations

1. Add 1 cup chopped green pepper and sauté along with the onion, garlic and turkey.
2. Season the stock with: 1/2 teaspoon thyme
    1/4 teaspoon pepper
    1/4 teaspoon cinnamon
    1/4 teaspoon allspice
3. When the rice is done, add 1 can (8-ounce) stewed tomatoes. Omit the raisins.

Lemon Turkey with Cinnamon

Serves 6

4 cups uncooked turkey,
    cut into 1-inch chunks
3 tablespoons olive oil
3 medium onions, chopped
2 cloves garlic, minced
2/3 cup canned tomatoes, drained
3 tablespoons tomato paste
2 cinnamon sticks, broken in half
2 medium lemons, coarsely chopped
    (skin and all)
1½ teaspoons oregano
1/8 teaspoon allspice
3 cups turkey stock
1/2 cup flour
3 tablespoons olive oil
salt and pepper to taste
1/2 cup grated Parmesan cheese

1. In a large sauce pan, heat 3 tablespoons olive oil and sauté onion until golden. Stir in garlic and cook an additional minute.

2. Reduce heat and stir in tomatoes, tomato paste, cinnamon sticks, chopped lemons, oregano and all-spice. Simmer about 5 minutes.

3. Add stock and simmer, covered, for 1¼ hours.

4. While sauce is simmering, heat 3 tablespoons olive oil in large skillet over high heat. Dredge turkey pieces in flour, shake off excess, and quickly stir-fry in small batches until lightly browned. Do not overcook. Remove from heat and set aside.

5. Add turkey to sauce and simmer, uncovered, an additional 15 minutes.

6. Adjust seasonings to taste and remove lemon pieces and cinnamon sticks.

7. Serve over your favorite pasta and garnish with Parmesan cheese.

Spinach noodles make this a very colorful dish.

Stir-Fry Turkey and Cashews

Serves 4

This is made with hoisin sauce which adds a piquant flavor to this stir-fry. You'll find hoisin sauce in the gourmet section of supermarkets and in Oriental grocery stores.

3 cups small uncooked turkey pieces (white meat is best)
2 tablespoons soy sauce
1 tablespoon dry sherry
1/2 teaspoon sugar (optional)
1 cup unsalted cashew nuts
2 tablespoons vegetable oil
1 tablespoon hoisin sauce
3 green onions, chopped
3 cups hot cooked rice

1. In medium bowl, combine turkey, soy sauce, sherry and sugar. Set aside. (This can be done early in the day, covered and refrigerated.)

2. In a skillet or wok, stir-fry cashews in hot oil over high heat for 1 to 2 minutes or until browned. Lift out with slotted spoon and drain on paper towel.

3. Add turkey mixture to skillet and stir-fry for several minutes. Do not overcook.

4. Stir in hoisin sauce and cashews. Sprinkle with green onions.

5. Serve at once with rice.

This is also delicious with vegetables added. Pea pods are especially good along with green beans, broccoli and mushrooms. Remove the turkey after step #3. Stir-fry the vegetables until tender-crisp and return the turkey to the skillet and continue as directed.

Szecheuan Turkey and Eggplant

This is a spicy-hot and delicious dish

> **2 cups uncooked turkey pieces**
> **1/4 cup turkey stock**
> **2 tablespoons vegetable oil for stir-fry**
> **1/4 pound ground pork**
> **1 tablespoon minced garlic**
> **1 tablespoon minced ginger root**
> **1 medium eggplant, peeled and julienned**
> **2 tablespoons soy sauce**
> **1 tablespoon hot bean paste (soy bean paste with chili, found in Chinese grocery)**
> **1 teaspoon honey**
> **1 teaspoon sesame oil**
> **1/2 tablespoon vinegar (brown Chinese preferred)**
> **1 tablespoon wine**
> **2 green onions, chopped**

1. Heat oil in wok or skillet and stir-fry pork until all pink is gone.

2. Add turkey, garlic and ginger and stir-fry quickly (about 2 minutes).

3. Add eggplant and stir about 1 minute.

4. Add soy sauce, stock, bean paste, and honey, stirring slowly about 5 minutes until all liquid is absorbed and eggplant is soft.

5. Sprinkle in sesame oil, vinegar, wine and green onions and mix well.

6. Serve over hot, cooked rice.

Crepes

3/4 cup flour
1/2 teaspoon salt
1 teaspoon baking powder
2 eggs
2/3 cup milk
1/3 cup water

1. Put all ingredients into blender and blend until smooth.

2. Refrigerate 1 to 2 hours.

3. Cook in 5-inch skillet or electric crepe pan, using small amount (2 tablespoons) of batter at a time.

If using a 5-inch skillet, use moderate heat. Grease with a few drops of oil, add a small amount of batter, tip the skillet and let the batter spread over the bottom. When lightly browned, reverse it and brown the other side. These crepes can be frozen (with wax paper between each one) and used as needed.

Variation: Corn Crepes

This variation can be used in Mexican dishes in place of flour or corn tortillas.

2 eggs
3/4 cup milk
1 tablespoon melted butter
1/2 cup masa harina (dehydrated masa flour)
2 tablespoons regular all-purpose wheat flour
1/4 teaspoon salt

1. Put all ingredients into blender and blend until smooth.

2. Refrigerate 1 to 2 hours.

3. Use 2 tablespoons of batter for each crepe, about 5 inches in diameter.

4. Cook in 5-inch skillet or in crepe pan.

Turkey Crepes

4 cups cooked turkey pieces, finely chopped
2¾ cups turkey stock, heated
3 tablespoons butter
2 cups sliced fresh mushrooms
4 tablespoons butter
5 tablespoons flour
1/2 teaspoon salt
1/8 teaspoon pepper
dash of nutmeg
1/4 cup cream
1 cup grated Swiss cheese, divided
12 crepes (see page 138)

1. Heat 3 tablespoons butter in skillet and sauté mushrooms. Add turkey, heat, and set aside.
2. Melt 4 tablespoons butter in sauce pan and stir in flour. Cook, stirring constantly for 3 minutes but do not brown.
3. Remove from heat and add stock and seasonings, stirring until sauce thickens. Return to heat and boil 1 minute.
4. Reduce heat and gradually stir in cream. Do not boil.
5. Remove from heat and add 3/4 cup cheese.
6. Mix 2/3 of the sauce with the turkey mixture.
7. Fill lower third of each crepe with 2 to 3 tablespoons of the turkey mixture.
8. Roll crepes and place seam side down close together in buttered shallow baking dish.
9. Spoon reserved sauce over crepes and sprinkle with remaining cheese.
10. Bake 350 degrees for 30 minutes.

Turkey-Vegetable Crepes

Serves 4

**3 cups cooked turkey pieces,
    finely chopped**
**3 cups Cheddar cheese, shredded
    and divided**
**1 can (8-ounce) water chestnuts,
    drained and sliced**
1/3 cup chopped green pepper
1/3 cup chopped celery
1/3 cup chopped fresh mushrooms
1 medium onion, chopped
1/2 teaspoon salt
1/4 teaspoon pepper
1½ teaspoon Worcestershire sauce
8 to 10 prepared crepes (see page 138)

1. Combine all ingredients except 2 cups cheese and crepes.
2. Fill lower third of each crepe with mixture.
3. Roll crepe and place seam side down in buttered shallow baking dish.
4. Cover and bake 350 degrees for 30 minutes.
5. Sprinkle with 2 cups cheese. Bake additional 10 minutes.

140

Mexican Turkey Crepes

Serves 6

**3 cups cooked turkey pieces,
    finely chopped**
2 cups sour cream
2 garlic cloves, minced
1½ teaspoons chili powder
1 teaspoon salt
1 teaspoon ground cumin
**1 can (4-ounce) diced green
    chiles, drained**
2 cups shredded Jack cheese
**1½ cups thinly sliced green onion
    (tops included)**
12 crepes (see page 138)
1 cup shredded Cheddar cheese
2 tomatoes, chopped
1 cup guacamole

1. Stir together turkey, sour cream, garlic, chili powder, salt, cumin, chiles, Jack cheese, and green onion.
2. Spoon 1/2 cup of mixture down center of each crepe and roll up to enclose.
3. Place crepes, seam side down, in buttered shallow baking dish. (Can be frozen at this point.)
4. Bake, covered, at 375 degrees 20 to 30 minutes.
5. Uncover, sprinkle with Cheddar cheese and bake 5 to 10 minutes longer.
6. Pass the chopped tomato and guacamole as garnish.

Brandy Cream Turkey Crepes

Serves 8

4 cups cooked turkey pieces,
   finely chopped
1 cup turkey stock
3 tablespoons butter
1 medium onion, finely chopped
1 large clove garlic, minced
2 cups sliced fresh mushrooms
3 tablespoons butter
3 tablespoons flour
1/8 teaspoon nutmeg
1/2 teaspoon thyme

1/2 teaspoon marjoram
dash of cayenne pepper
salt and pepper to taste
   (white pepper is best)
3 tablespoons brandy, divided
3 egg yolks
1 cup half and half
juice of 1/2 lemon
1 cup Swiss cheese
8 to 12 prepared crepes (see page 138)

1. Heat butter in skillet and sauté onion and garlic until golden.

2. Stir in mushrooms and cook about 3 minutes. Add turkey.

3. Melt butter in sauce pan and stir in flour, cooking for 3 minutes. Do not brown.

4. Slowly add stock, stirring constantly, and cook until sauce thickens.

5. Stir in seasonings and 2 tablespoons brandy.

6. Beat egg yolks with half and half and whisk them slowly into the sauce. Do not boil.

7. Mix 2/3 of the sauce with turkey filling.

8. Add remaining brandy and the lemon juice to the other 1/3 of sauce.

9. Fill lower third of each crepe with 3 tablespoons turkey filling.

10. Roll crepes and place seam side down close together in buttered shallow baking dish. Spoon reserved sauce over crepes. Sprinkle with cheese.

11. Bake 350 degrees for 20 minutes.

Turkey Spinach Crepes

2 cups cooked turkey pieces, finely chopped
2 tablespoons butter
1/2 cup chopped onion
1/4 pound fresh mushrooms, chopped
1 package (10-ounce) frozen spinach, thawed and squeezed dry
1 package (3-ounce) cream cheese
1/2 cup sour cream
1 to 2 teaspoons Dijon mustard
1/4 teaspoon nutmeg
salt and pepper to taste
12 prepared crepes (see page 138)

1. Melt butter in a large sauce pan and sauté onions until tender crisp.
2. Add mushrooms and sauté until done.
3. Add spinach and turkey to onion mixture.
4. Combine cream cheese, sour cream, mustard and seasonings.
5. Add to spinach mixture.
6. Fill lower third of each crepe with mixture.
7. Roll crepe and place seam side down in buttered, shallow baking dish.
8. Pour cheese sauce over the crepes.
9. Bake 350 degrees for 30 minutes or until hot.

Cheese Sauce

1 cup Velouté sauce (see page 75)
1 cup grated Swiss cheese
dash nutmeg

Turkey Tacos

Serves 6

1½ pounds ground turkey
1 small onion, chopped
1 tablespoon vegetable oil
1/2 teaspoon oregano
1 tablespoon chili powder
1 teaspoon salt
1/8 teaspoon pepper
1 teaspoon paprika
1/4 teaspoon garlic powder
6 or more taco shells
2 tomatoes, chopped
1/2 head Iceberg lettuce, shredded
1 cup shredded Cheddar cheese
bottled taco sauce
guacamole

Aye yi-yi-yi!

1. Sauté turkey and onion in oil. Add oregano, chili powder, salt, pepper, paprika and garlic powder.

2. Cook, uncovered, stirring occasionally until moisture has evaporated.

3. Heat taco shells in 350 degree oven for 5 minutes.

4. Spoon turkey mixture into taco shells and top as desired with tomatoes, lettuce and cheese. Pass the taco sauce and guacamole.

You could also serve chopped green onions, chopped black olives, chopped green chiles, chopped avocado and salsa as toppings along with the above.

Turkey, Sausage and Spinach Pie

Serves 10

1 pound ground turkey
1/2 pound pork sausage
6 eggs, beaten (reserve 1 egg yolk)
2 packages (10-ounce each) frozen
   chopped spinach, thawed and
   squeezed dry
1 pound Mozzarella cheese, shredded
2/3 cup Ricotta cheese
1 teaspoon salt
1/4 teaspoon pepper
pastry for two 9-inch pie crusts
   (see page 182)
2 teaspoons water

Be adventurous!

1. Cook turkey and sausage until browned (10 minutes). Drain off excess fat.

2. In large bowl, combine eggs (except 1 yolk), turkey mixture, spinach, cheeses, and salt and pepper. Set aside.

3. Divide pastry into balls, using 2/3 of pastry for one ball and remaining 1/3 for second ball.

4. Roll large ball into 16-inch circle and press into 9-inch springform pan. Trim pastry edge even with rim of pan.

5. Spoon turkey mixture into pan and fold edge of pastry over filling.

6. Combine 2 teaspoons water and reserved egg yolk and brush some onto the folded edge of pastry.

7. Roll remaining pastry ball into 9-inch circle and place over mixture, pressing around edge to seal. Cut out small circle in middle of pastry.

8. Brush top with egg yolk mixture.

9. Bake in 375 degree oven about 1¼ hours or until piecrust is golden.

10. Cool pie in pan on wire rack 10 minutes for easier serving.

11. Loosen crust from side of pan. Carefully remove pie and cut in wedges to serve.

Sweet and Sour Turkey Meat Balls

Serves 6

1½ pounds ground turkey
1 small onion, minced
1 egg, beaten
1/2 cup seasoned dried bread crumbs
salt and pepper to taste
1 can (16-ounce) tomatoes, cut up
1/4 cup diced green pepper
1/2 cup diced celery
1/2 cup diced onion
1/2 teaspoon cinnamon
1/4 teaspoon ground cloves
1/4 teaspoon dry mustard
1/4 cup vinegar
1/4 cup brown sugar
hot cooked noodles or rice

1. Combine turkey, onion, egg, bread crumbs, salt and pepper. Shape into 1-inch meatballs.

2. Bake meatballs in 325 degree oven for 20 minutes, or until done.

3. While meatballs are baking, combine remaining ingredients, except noodles, and simmer until vegetables are tender.

4. Add meatballs and serve over hot noodles or rice.

Spinach noodles make a very colorful dish.

Spaghetti Pie

1 pound ground turkey
1/4 pound Italian sausage
1/2 cup chopped onion
1/4 cup chopped green pepper
1 teaspoon garlic salt
1 teaspoon oregano
1 can (8-ounce) tomatoes
1 can (6-ounce) tomato paste
6 ounces spaghetti, cooked and
**   drained**
2 tablespoons butter
1/3 cup grated Parmesan cheese
2 eggs, slightly beaten
1 cup cottage cheese (Ricotta is
**   even better)**
1 cup grated Mozzarella cheese

1. Combine turkey, sausage, onion, green pepper and seasonings. Sauté until meat is browned and vegetables are limp.

2. Add tomatoes and tomato paste and simmer.

3. Combine spaghetti, butter, Parmesan cheese and eggs.

4. Grease a 10-inch pie pan and spread the spaghetti mixture into pan, similar to a pie shell.

5. Place cottage cheese in bottom and cover with meat mixture.

6. Bake, uncovered, 350 degrees for 30 minutes.

7. Add Mozzarella cheese and bake an additional 5 minutes or until cheese melts.

8. Serve in wedges as you would a piece of pie.

Turkey Meatballs, Mexican Flavor

Serves 6

2 pounds ground turkey
2 eggs, beaten
1/3 cup minced onion
1/3 cup milk
2 teaspoons salt
1/2 teaspoon pepper
1½ cups soft bread crumbs

1. Combine eggs with onion, milk, salt, pepper, and bread crumbs.

2. Blend in turkey (hands work well here). Shape into 1-inch balls and place on greased baking sheet.

3. Bake 20 to 25 minutes 375 degrees until browned.

4. Prepare sauce (see below). Pour sauce over meatballs and serve.

Cheese Sauce

2 tablespoons vegetable oil
1 large onion, chopped
1 large can (7-ounce) diced
    green chiles
1 teaspoon salt
1 small can (5-ounce) evaporated milk
2 cups grated Cheddar cheese

Aye yi-yi-yi!

1. In a sauce pan, heat oil and sauté onion until very soft.

2. Add chiles and salt. Cook until juices evaporate (about 5 minutes).

3. Add milk and stir until slightly thickened. Do not boil.

4. Remove from heat and add cheese. Stir until cheese melts.

Turkey Loaf with Sweet 'N Sour Sauce

Serves 6

2 pounds ground turkey
2 eggs
2/3 cup chili sauce
1/2 cup chopped onion
1 teaspoon salt

1/2 teaspoon pepper
1/2 teaspoon marjoram
1/4 teaspoon thyme
1 cup cornflakes
Sweet 'n Sour Sauce (see below)

1. Beat eggs lightly. Stir in chili sauce, onion and seasonings.

2. Blend in cornflakes and turkey (hands work well). Press into 9x9 shallow casserole.

3. Bake, uncovered, at 350 degrees about 30 minutes.

4. Spoon sauce over loaf. Bake additional 15 minutes.

Sweet 'N Sour Sauce

1/4 cup brown sugar, firmly packed
2 tablespoons cornstarch
1/2 teaspoon salt
**1 can (10½-ounce) pineapple chunks,
   drained (reserve syrup)**

1/3 cup cider vinegar
1 tablespoon soy sauce
1 large green pepper, thinly sliced
1/4 cup chopped onion

1. In medium sauce pan, combine sugar, cornstarch and salt.

2. Add water to reserved pineapple syrup to make 1 cup. Gradually stir into sugar mixture.

3. Stir in vinegar and soy sauce.

4. Cook and stir over low heat until thickened and clear.

5. Add pineapple chunks, green pepper, and onion.

6. Pour over turkey loaf.

We suggest serving hot, cooked rice with this turkey loaf.

Ground Turkey Enchiladas

Serves 6

1½ pounds ground turkey
1 onion, chopped
1 teaspoon salt
1/4 teaspoon garlic powder
1/3 cup bottled taco sauce
1 can (1 pound) refried beans
1 can (2½-ounce) chopped black olives, drained
1 dozen flour tortillas
vegetable oil for frying
2 cans (10-ounce each) enchilada sauce
1 cup grated Cheddar cheese
sour cream
canned salsa

1. Sauté turkey and onion in 2 tablespoons vegetable oil. Add salt, garlic, taco sauce, beans, and olives. Simmer until bubbly.

2. Fry tortilla shells quickly in hot oil and drain well on paper towels. Shells should still be soft.

3. Pour 1 can enchilada sauce into shallow baking dish.

4. Roll 1/3 cup filling into each shell. Place seam side down in sauce. Pour remaining sauce over and top with cheese.

5. Bake 350 degrees for 30 minutes until hot and bubbly.

6. Serve with sour cream and salsa.

Aye yi-yi-yi!

Turkey Shish-Kebabs

Serves 8

**4 cups uncooked turkey, cut into
    1-inch chunks (dark meat can
    be used, too)**
**2 large green peppers, cut into
    1-inch chunks**
3 cups pineapple chunks (fresh is best)
16 large whole fresh mushrooms
8 cherry tomatoes
**1 cup thick and spicy Italian or
    French dressing of your choice**

1. Thread turkey, green pepper, pineapple and mushrooms onto 8 skewers.

2. Brush all sides generously with dressing.

3. Broil or grill over hot coals, turning and basting often with dressing.

4. Put tomato on at the last minute, just long enough to heat through.

Oven Barbequed Legs

Serves 6

6 turkey legs (or thighs)
1/2 cup turkey stock
1/2 cup flour
2 teaspoons salt
1 teaspoon chili powder
1/2 teaspoon pepper
1/2 cup vegetable oil
1/2 cup barbeque sauce

1. Combine flour, salt, chili powder and pepper.

2. Dredge turkey legs in flour mixture.

3. Brown in hot oil on all sides and remove to shallow baking dish.

4. Mix barbeque sauce and stock and pour over turkey legs.

5. Cover and bake 325 degrees for 1 hour.

6. Uncover and bake an additional 1 hour, basting often.

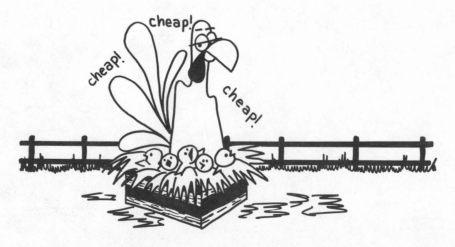

Turkey and Dumplings

2 turkey hindquarters (2 legs and 2 thighs)
2 quarts turkey stock
2 carrots, peeled and chopped
2 potatoes, peeled and cubed
1 large onion, chopped
1 clove garlic, minced
1/4 cup flour
1/4 cup water
biscuit mix for dumplings

1. In large kettle, simmer the hindquarters in stock until meat is tender (about 1½ hours).

2. Remove hindquarters and debone, reserving meat in large chunks.

3. Add vegetables to stock and cook until tender (about 15 minutes).

4. Combine flour and water into smooth paste. Add some hot stock to the flour mixture to heat and return to the stock, stirring constantly. Heat and stir to thicken.

5. Prepare dumplings according to package directions.

6. Return turkey chunks to gravy. Drop dumplings into gravy and cook for 10 minutes uncovered and 10 minutes covered.

This is a hearty and nutritious meal that is guaranteed to make your family happy on a cold winter's night.

Turkey and White Bean Casserole

Serves 6

2 large turkey hindquarters (2 legs and 2 thighs)
1/2 pound dry white beans
1/2 cup dry white wine (or turkey stock)
6 to 8 slices bacon, diced
2 large onions, chopped
3 cloves garlic, minced
4 medium-size carrots, sliced into 1-inch chunks
2 stalks celery, sliced into 1/4-inch slices
1 can (14¼-ounce) pear-shaped tomatoes
1½ teaspoons rosemary leaves
salt and pepper to taste

1. Several hours before serving, soak and cook dry beans as directed on package. Drain.

2. Brown turkey in 6-quart casserole or Dutch oven in hot 450 degree oven for 25 minutes. Remove fat.

3. Pour wine over turkey, cover and bake 350 degrees for 1 hour.

4. In large frying pan, cook bacon until crisp. Remove, drain and set aside.

5. Sauté onion and garlic in pan drippings.

6. Add carrots, celery, tomatoes, rosemary and cooked beans. Heat to boiling, season to taste with salt and pepper.

7. After turkey has baked 1 hour, pour hot bean mixture over. Cover and continue baking for 1 additional hour.

8. Let stand 15 minutes before serving. Garnish with bacon. (The bacon is very important to the flavor of the casserole so be sure to include.)

If there are any leftovers, debone the turkey, add turkey stock, and make a delicious soup for another meal. This would cook up beautifully in the crock pot.

Summer Garden Turkey

2 turkey hindquarters (2 legs and 2 thighs)
1/2 cup vegetable oil
1/3 cup red wine vinegar
2 tablespoons chopped green onions
3 cloves garlic, pressed
1 tablespoon Dijon mustard
1 teaspoon honey
1/2 teaspoon oregano
1/2 teaspoon basil
1/2 teaspoon tarragon
salt and pepper to taste
3 cups cooked rice
4 to 6 cups lightly steamed vegetables of your choice (sugar-snap peas,
carrots, asparagus, zucchini, green beans, broccoli, onions)

1. In a sauce pan, combine oil, vinegar, green onions, garlic, mustard, honey, oregano, basil, tarragon, salt and pepper. Heat.

2. Place turkey on rack in shallow roasting pan and roast 325 degrees about 2 hours or until tender.

3. Baste turkey hindquarters with some of the sauce while cooking.

4. Heat the rice and steam vegetables until tender-crisp.

5. Toss the rice and vegetables together with remaining sauce.

6. Arrange vegetables and rice combination on platter and top with carved pieces of turkey.

Oven-Baked Turkey Legs

4 turkey legs (or legs and thighs)
1 cup water
1/2 cup soy sauce
1/2 cup thinly sliced green onion
1 clove garlic, minced
1/2 teaspoon cinnamon
1/2 teaspoon ginger
1/4 teaspoon allspice
1/4 teaspoon crushed anise seeds
1/8 teaspoon ground cloves
1/4 cup cornstarch
1/4 cup water

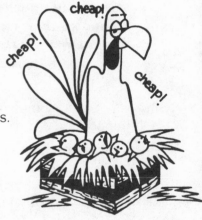

1. Place turkey legs in roasting pan.
2. Stir together the water, soy sauce, green onions, garlic and seasonings.
3. Pour over turkey. Cover and chill 4 hours or overnight. Turn several times.
4. Bake, covered, 350 degrees for 1½ hours. Turn halfway through baking.
5. Uncover and bake 45 minutes longer, turning several times.
6. Lift legs onto serving dish.
7. Skim fat from pan juices and pour juices into saucepan.
8. Stir together the cornstarch and water and add to pan juices to thicken.
9. Heat and stir until sauce boils and thickens.
10. Pass the sauce at the table.

If you have a jar of Chinese Five-Spice, use 1½ teaspoons in place of the seasonings in this recipe.

Turkey Cacciatore

6 turkey thighs or drumsticks
1/2 cup turkey stock
1/4 cup butter
3 large onions, chopped
4 cloves garlic, minced
2 green peppers, chopped
1/2 pound fresh mushrooms, sliced
2 tablespoons flour
1 can (8-ounce) tomato sauce
1 can (16-ounce) stewed tomatoes
1/2 cup dry red wine

1/2 teaspoon salt
1 teaspoon dry basil
1 teaspoon thyme
1 teaspoon oregano
3 teaspoons sugar
1/8 teaspoon ground allspice
2 whole bay leaves
1/3 cup grated Parmesan cheese
parsley-buttered spaghetti
additional grated Parmesan cheese

1. Brown turkey in hot 450 degree oven for 25 minutes. Remove as browned.

2. In large skillet, melt butter and sauté onions until limp. Add garlic, green peppers, and mushrooms. Cook and stir until well done.

3. Sprinkle flour over mixture in skillet, mixing in well.

4. Add tomato sauce, tomatoes, wine, stock and seasonings. Bring to boil, stirring.

5. Pour off fat from turkey pan. Return turkey to pan and pour sauce over, pushing turkey pieces down into sauce.

6. Cover, reduce heat to 325 degrees, and simmer about 30 minutes.

7. Uncover and cook an additional 1 to 1½ hours.

8. Transfer to serving dish, discard bay leaves, sprinkle with Parmesan cheese and serve with parsley-buttered spaghetti.

9. Pass more Parmesan cheese at the table.

Parsley-Buttered Spaghetti

1. Cook 1 pound spaghetti as directed on package.

2. Rinse, drain and turn into warm dish.

3. Mix 2 tablespoons melted butter and 2 tablespoons parsley.

4. Pour over spaghetti and toss lightly.

Caribbean Turkey Stew

4 turkey wings (or legs)
4 turkey thighs
3½ cups turkey stock
1/2 teaspoon pepper
1½ teaspoon salt, divided
3 tablespoons vegetable oil
1 medium green pepper, diced
1 medium onion, diced
1 garlic clove, minced
2 tablespoons flour
1 can (10½-ounce) tomato puree
2 tablespoons red wine vinegar
3 large potatoes, peeled and cut into chunks
1 jar (3-ounce) pimiento-stuffed olives, drained
1 package (10-ounce) frozen peas

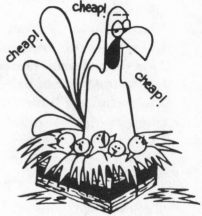

1. Cut each wing at joints and discard end piece. Sprinkle wings and thighs with salt and pepper and brown in hot oil. Remove.

2. In drippings, sauté green pepper, onion, and garlic until tender crisp.

3. Reduce heat, stir in flour and blend well. Stir in stock, tomato puree, vinegar, and 1 teaspoon salt.

4. Return wings and thighs to pan and heat to boiling. Reduce heat to low, cover, and simmer 2 hours, basting occasionally. Remove meat and set aside.

5. Skim fat from liquid in pan. Add potatoes and heat to boiling. Simmer 30 minutes.

6. Debone meat in large chunks. Return meat to pan and add olives and peas. Cook 10 minutes longer to heat through.

Hawaiian Turkey Wings

Serves 4

4 turkey wings
1 large can (15-ounce) tomato sauce
1 teaspoon salt
1/4 cup vinegar
1 teaspoon chili powder
1/2 teaspoon liquid smoke
1/4 teaspoon pepper
1/8 teaspoon garlic powder
1 can (8-ounce) pineapple slices
(reserve juice)

1. Remove small end of wing and discard.
2. Bake wings 450 degrees for 20 minutes to brown.
3. In a saucepan, combine tomato sauce, salt, vinegar, chili powder, liquid smoke, pepper, garlic powder, and 1/4 cup pineapple syrup. Heat to boiling.
4. Place wings in covered baking dish and cover with sauce.
5. Bake 350 degrees for 1 hour, basting occasionally.
6. Uncover, skim off any fat on sauce, and garnish with pineapple slices.
7. Bake, uncovered, for 15 minutes.

This is very good served with rice. You can also use thighs and legs in place of wings if you wish, but increase baking time to 2 hours.

Pot Roast Turkey

Serves 4

2 large turkey hindquarters
    (two legs and 2 thighs)
1 cup dry red wine (or turkey stock)
2 tablespoons vegetable oil
2 large onions, chopped
2 large cloves garlic, minced
1 can (10¾-ounce) mushroom soup
1 teaspoon dry basil
1 teaspoon thyme
1 teaspoon sage
1 tablespoon Dijon mustard
8 small whole carrots
8 small potatoes
8 small boiling onions
3 tablespoons cornstarch
3 tablespoons water
salt and pepper to taste

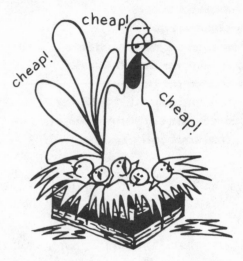

1. Brown turkey in large casserole in hot 450 degree oven for 25 minutes. Remove fat.

2. In large skillet, sauté onions and garlic in oil. Add wine, soup, seasonings, and mustard. Bring to boil.

3. Pour sauce over turkey, cover, and bake 325 degrees for 1 hour.

4. Add the carrots, potatoes and onions, pushing vegetables down into juices.

5. Cover and bake additional 1 hour.

6. With slotted spoon, lift vegetables and meat onto serving plate and keep warm.

7. If necessary, skim fat from cooking liquid. Add mixture of cornstarch and water and blend until smooth.

8. Spoon small amount of sauce over meat and vegetables and pass remaining sauce at the table. Serve with hot biscuits.

The sauce (as made in step #2) is absolutely delicious used as a gravy for any leftover turkey.

Curried Turkey Hindquarter

Serves 6

2 turkey hindquarters
   (2 legs and 2 thighs)
3 cups turkey stock
2 medium onions, chopped
4 garlic cloves, minced
1/4 cup vegetable oil
1 tablespoon turmeric
1 tablespoon ground cumin
2 tablespoons ground coriander
1/2 tablespoon red pepper
1 tablespoon ginger
8 cloves
1 stick cinnamon
salt to taste
1 cup apple juice
3 tablespoons cornstarch
2 tablespoons water

1. Brown turkey hindquarters in hot 450 degree oven for about 25 minutes.

2. Heat oil in skillet and sauté onion, garlic and spices (except cloves and cinnamon) for about 5 minutes.

3. Stir in apple juice, stock, cloves and cinnamon. Pour sauce over hindquarters and bake 2 hours at 350 degrees.

4. Remove turkey and keep warm. Skim off and discard any surface fat. Remove cloves and cinnamon.

5. Blend cornstarch with water and stir into sauce in pan. Cook and stir until sauce boils and thickens.

6. Debone turkey and return to pan.

Serve with hot, cooked rice and offer condiments such as yogurt, salted peanuts, coconut, raisins, chopped green onions, chopped apple, and chopped banana.

Roasted Turkey Breast

1 turkey breast (size depends on the number of people to serve)
seasoning salt

1. Season breast well. Place skin side up in roasting pan.
2. Bake 325 degrees 1 to 2 hours, depending on size of breast. (Meat thermometer will register 180 degrees when done.)

Marinades for Turkey Breast

Teriyaki Marinade

1/2 cup vegetable oil
1 cup soy sauce
3 tablespoons brown sugar
3 cloves garlic, minced
1 tablespoon chopped fresh
ginger root
3 tablespoons sherry

1. Combine all ingredients and pour into sturdy plastic bag.
2. Add turkey, seal bag, and marinate breast 4 hours or overnight, turning occasionally.
3. Bake as directed above.

Hot and Spicy Marinade

2/3 cup vegetable oil
1/2 cup lemon juice
3 cloves garlic, crushed
1/2 teaspoon seasoning salt
1/4 teaspoon pepper
1 can (8-ounce) tomato sauce
1 can (3½-ounce) diced jalapeno
peppers, drained
1 teaspoon garlic salt
1/2 teaspoon ground cumin

1. Combine oil, lemon juice, garlic, salt and pepper. Pour over turkey.
2. Cover and refrigerate at least 8 hours or overnight, turning occasionally.
3. Pour off marinade and combine it with tomato sauce, jalapeno peppers, garlic salt and ground cumin.
4. Baste turkey often with marinade while roasting.

Roasted Turkey Breast, continued

Lemon-Thyme Marinade

1/2 cup vegetable oil
1/4 cup lemon juice
1 teaspoon salt
1 teaspoon thyme
2 tablespoons minced onion
1 clove garlic, minced

1. Combine ingredients; pour over turkey. Cover and refrigerate for several hours.

2. Baste breast frequently during roasting with marinade. (This is also a good basting if you want to barbeque the turkey breast in a covered barbeque.)

Greek Marinade

2 teaspoons salt
1/2 teaspoon pepper
3 cloves garlic, minced
1/2 cup olive oil
1/2 cup white wine vinegar
2 medium tomatoes, chopped
2 medium green peppers, chopped
1/4 cup chopped parsley
1 can (2½-ounce) sliced ripe olives, drained

1. Mix salt, pepper and garlic together and rub thoroughly into turkey breast.

2. Combine oil, vinegar, tomato, green pepper, parsley and olives.

3. Pour over turkey breast and refrigerate overnight, turning occasionally.

4. Bake the breast in a deep baking dish so that marinade all but covers.

5. When serving, use slotted spoon and cover turkey slices with hot vegetables from the marinade.

Stuffed Roasted Turkey Breast

10-pound turkey breast
1/2 cup butter, melted
1 large piece of cheese cloth
salt and pepper to taste
your favorite turkey dressing
2 large carrots, coarsely chopped

1. Remove both turkey lobes from breast bone. Carefully remove skin from turkey lobes. (Reserve carcass for stock.)
2. Dip cheese cloth in melted butter and spread it out in baking pan.
3. Brush melted butter over the turkey skin and spread it (outer side down) on the cheese cloth.
4. Season turkey lobes with salt and pepper, brush with butter, and arrange smooth side down onto skin.
5. Spoon stuffing over meat. Bring cheese cloth up over, wrapping like a package. Tie with string to secure.
6. Turn the turkey, skin side up, in roasting pan and arrange carrots alongside.
7. Place turkey in lower-middle level of oven and roast 325 degrees for 2 hours or until thermometer reaches 158-160 degrees. Baste often with melted butter.
8. Remove turkey from oven and place on heated platter. Let it rest for 20 minutes before slicing. Remove cheese cloth.
9. Serve with gravy.

Gravy

1. Place roasting pan on top of stove. Remove some of the excess fat and carrots. (Don't be concerned about removing all the fat. You need some of the fat to absorb the flour.)
2. Over medium heat, add about 1/2 cup flour and whisk until completely blended with pan juices. Be sure to cook flour at least 2 minutes. (Plan on 1/2 cup flour to 8 cups liquid.)
3. While stirring constantly, slowly add liquid to make gravy (turkey stock, milk, cream, mild vegetable juices, water, or any combination including white wine and brandy) until you have reached desired consistency and amount of gravy.

Foil Baked Turkey Breast

Serves 4

1 half-breast of turkey (about
    2 to 3 pounds)
salt to taste
2 tablespoons butter
2 tablespoons grated Parmesan cheese
2 tablespoons flour
1/4 teaspoon dill weed
1/4 teaspoon crumbled basil weeds
1/8 teaspoon pepper
1 tablespoon cornstarch
1 tablespoon white wine

1. Lightly salt the underside of the turkey breast.

2. Combine butter, cheese, flour and seasonings. Spread over skin of turkey.

3. Enclose breast in sheet of heavy foil. Place in shallow pan.

4. Bake 350 degrees for 1 hour.

5. Remove breast; pour off juices into sauce pan.

6. Blend cornstarch with wine and add to juices. Cook and stir until mixture boils and thickens. Add water if needed to obtain right consistency for a sauce.

7. Slice breast and serve with sauce.

Turkey Breast with Crust

Serves 8

1 whole turkey breast (about
    6-8 pounds), boned, rolled and tied
salt and pepper
1/4 cup melted butter, divided
1/4 cup dry white wine
1½ cups grated Gruyere cheese
    (Swiss or Jack is also good)
1 tablespoon Dijon mustard
1 cup heavy cream

1. Place turkey, skin side up, on rack in roasting pan.

2. Sprinkle lightly with salt and pepper and drizzle with 2 tablespoons butter.

3. Mix remaining butter with wine to use as a basting.

4. Roast, uncovered, 325 degrees for 25 minutes per pound (1½ to 2½ hours). Baste often.

5. Transfer roast from roasting pan to oven-proof platter. Sprinkle with 3/4 cup cheese and keep warm.

6. Skim fat from pan juices. Add mustard and cream to pan, scrapping all browned bits.

7. Set on high heat and bring to a boil, whisking constantly.

8. Remove and stir in remaining cheese and serve as a gravy for the roasted turkey breast.

Zenobia's Italian Turkey

This recipe came from Zenobia's, a wonderful pastry shop in Lake Grove, Oregon. Donna Zenobia-Saffir, the owner, shared it with us.

1 10- to 12-pound turkey
1/2 teaspoon thyme
2 peeled garlic cloves
1 onion, peeled and quartered
1/2 lemon, coarsely chopped, rind and all
1/2 orange, coarsely chopped, rind and all
1 crushed garlic clove
2 teaspoons Kitchen Bouquet®
8 slices bacon

1. Dry inside of turkey with paper towel. Sprinkle thyme inside turkey cavity.

2. Combine garlic cloves, onion, lemon and orange and put inside turkey cavity.

3. Do not truss turkey. Place it in a large roasting pan on its back.

4. Rub outside of turkey with crushed garlic and Kitchen Bouquet®. Lay strips of bacon over turkey breast.

5. Roast, uncovered, 400 degrees for 20 minutes. Lower temperature to 350 degrees and continue to roast uncovered for 2 to 3 hours or until turkey is done. Test doneness every 15 minutes after 2 hours roasting time.

6. Baste turkey every 20 minutes during roasting with basting sauce (see below).

Basting Sauce

1 cup Marsala wine
1/2 teaspoon thyme
2 tablespoons Kitchen Bouquet®

Combine all ingredients in a sauce pan or bowl.

The turkey will be a lovely brown color and the bacon will look burnt when the bird is done. Don't be alarmed, it's supposed to look that way.

Curry For A Crowd

Serves 60

You make this dish in four batches and then combine them. Each batch serves fifteen people, so if your guest list does not add up to sixty people, go ahead and make one or more batches of this curry.

**2 - 20 pound turkeys, roasted,
   deboned, and cubed (save
   drippings)**
5 quarts turkey stock
2 pounds butter
1-1/3 cup curry powder
5 cups flour
1 cup dried onion flakes
**1 box (11-ounce) seedless golden
   raisins**
plenty of hot cooked rice

1. Make curry sauce in four batches. For each batch:

   A. Bring to a boil 5 cups turkey stock plus 3 cups turkey drippings (add water to drippings to make 3 cups).

   B. In large skillet melt 1/2 pound (2 cubes) butter. Stir in 1/3 cup curry powder and 1¼ cup flour. Cook about 2 minutes.

   C. Stir hot stock into butter and cook, stirring constantly, until thickened.

2. After all four batches are made, stir in onion flakes and raisins. When sauce has cooled, add turkey. (This will fit into a large roasting pan.)

3. Bake, covered, 350 degrees for 2 hours. Serve over hot rice and offer condiments.

4. Suggested condiments:

chopped peanuts	banana pieces
chutney	chopped egg (hard-cooked)
coconut	mandarin oranges, chopped
raisins	chopped dates
chopped green onion	yogurt

It is best to make the sauce 1 to 3 days ahead of serving so the seasonings can blend. It can also be divided and stored in batches in the freezer.

Traditional Turkey Dinner

Roast Turkey with Dressing
Gravy

Green Vegetables   Sweet Potatoes

Cranberries   Fruit Salad

Pumpkin Dessert

How to Roast a Turkey

1. Free turkey legs from metal clasp (or whatever is confining them) and clean the turkey by letting cold water run through it. Dry it inside and out with paper towels.
2. Salt the cavities and fill them loosely with dressing. (Dressing will increase in bulk as it cooks.)
3. Secure the legs by whatever means necessary (metal clasp, skewers, etc.) and fill the neck cavity. Secure all openings.
4. Place the bird, breast side up, on a rack in a roasting pan, and cook according to time necessary for the weight of the bird. After the first hour, baste occasionally with pan drippings.
5. When done, let the turkey stand about 20 minutes before carving.

To Roast

Roast at 325 degrees.

For a bird up to 16 pounds: Stuffed: allow 20 to 25 minutes per pound.
Unstuffed: allow 15 minutes per pound.

For a bird over 16 pounds: Stuffed: allow 18 to 20 minutes per pound.
Unstuffed: allow 15 minutes per pound.

Variation

Prepare a large bird (20 to 25 pounds) and bake it 12 hours at 250 degrees. This is great to do late Christmas Eve and let it cook all night. It will be ready without fuss on Christmas Day. A word of caution. Be sure your oven temperature is accurate, because otherwise bacteria could be a problem.

Test for Doneness

Meat should be moist and firm. It should never be cooked until it "falls off the bone," but should not be pink either.

1. If using a meat thermometer, place it in the center part of the inner thigh muscle. Do not touch the bone. It will register 180 to 185 degrees when done.
2. Prick the thigh joint with a fork. If the juice runs clear, the turkey is done. This also adds extra juice to the pan drippings for the gravy.

How to Carve a Roasted Turkey

For best results, start with a carving board, a very sharp knife and a two-pronged carving fork. Remove the turkey from the oven (cover 2 oven mitts with plastic bags to lift the turkey from the roasting pan) and allow it to rest about 20 minutes for easier slicing. Place the bird breast-side up on the carving board in front of you with the legs on your right. Reverse if you're left-handed. Carve one side of the turkey at a time.

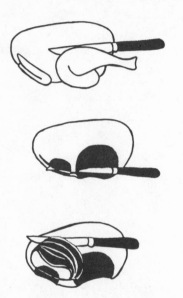

1. Start by slitting the skin between the thigh and the body and cut through to the joint. Remove the entire hindquarter by pulling it away from the body until the ball and socket hip joint is exposed. Use the point of the knife to disjoint the socket. Separate the thigh and the drumstuck at the joint and carve off some of the thigh meat, if desired.

2. Insert the fork into the largest part of the wing to steady the turkey. Starting just above the wing joint, make a long cut underneath the meat of the breast all the way to the breast bone. Remove the wing, using the same method as with the hindquarters in step 1.

3. Start at the front of the breast and slice straight down with an even stroke. When the knife reaches the cut above the wing bone, the meat will fall free. Continue slicing the white meat in this way but start cutting at a higher point each time.

4. When one side is completely carved, continue in the same manner on the other side.

We prefer to carve the bird in the kitchen and serve the meat neatly arranged on a platter garnished with parsley. This makes carving and serving easier and neater. While carving, have a large kettle available. As you carve, put all the excess bits and pieces of bone, skin, juices, etc. into the kettle in preparation for making stock (see page 19). This also makes clean-up much easier.

Turkey Dressing

Dressings are a special part of the menu and a must for the holiday meal. They are easily varied and adaptable to whatever you have on hand. Be creative. We feel the commercially prepared dressing breads are excellent and suggest using them as we have in our basic recipe. Allow approximately 3/4 cup stuffing per pound turkey. If you have extra stuffing, the best way to cook it is in a crock pot on low heat for as long as you cook the turkey. If you do not have a crock pot, put the stuffing in a greased covered casserole, add extra stock to moisten well, and bake 350 degrees for 1 hour.

Basic Recipe
10 to 12 pound turkey

1 large onion, chopped
2 large stalks celery, chopped
1 cube (1/4 pound) butter
1 package seasoned bread stuffing
turkey stock to moisten

1. Sauté onion and celery in butter.

2. In large bowl, add onion mixture to seasoned bread.

3. Moisten with turkey stock according to package directions.

4. Lightly spoon into salted turkey cavities (neck and body).

5. Close and secure all turkey openings.

Do not overstuff the turkey cavities as dressing will expand during cooking. Allow about 3/4 cup of stuffing per pound of turkey.

Experiment!

Variations for Turkey Dressing

1. Add chopped, cooked giblets to the dressing.

2. Add 1/2 to 1 pint lightly sauteed oysters. Use oyster liquid instead of turkey stock to moisten bread stuffing.

3. Sauté 1 large green pepper, chopped, along with the onion and celery.

4. Add 1 to 2 pounds sausage meat which has been sauteed and drained.

5. Add 1/2 to 1 pound fresh mushrooms which have been sauteed along with the onion and celery.

6. For extra crunch, add slivered or chopped almonds, brazil nuts, walnuts, pecans, or water chestnuts.

7. Add 1 cup of raisins.

8. Add chopped apples (peeled), prunes or apricots.

9. Finely chopped parsley adds another distinct flavor.

10. Chestnuts are a good addition. To prepare, cover chestnuts with water and boil 15 to 20 minutes. Drain, cut each one in half and scoop out meat with a spoon. (You can use French imported canned chestnuts if you wish.)

11. Beaten eggs can be added to help moisten the bread stuffing.

12. Cornbread can be used along with or instead of seasoned bread stuffing.

> 2 cups flour
> 1/2 cup sugar
> 8 teaspoons baking powder
> 1½ teaspoons salt
> 2 cups yellow cornmeal
> 4 eggs
> 2 cups milk
> 1/2 cup vegetable oil

1. Sift dry ingredients. Beat eggs and add milk and oil.

2. Add egg mixture to dry ingredients and mix until moistened.

3. Grease two 9x9x2 pans, add batter and bake 425 degrees for 30 to 40 minutes. Bread will be overcooked.

4. Allow bread to cool, then break into 1-inch chunks and leave out, uncovered, to dry overnight.

5. Season with poultry spice to taste before adding to the basic recipe.

Turkey Gravy

Making gravy is really not the hard job that so many cooks seem to think it is. It can be done in one pan and very simply. Don't worry about it.

1. Remove the turkey to a carving board or serving dish. (Cover 2 oven mitts with plastic bags to lift the turkey from the oven roasting pan.)
2. Place roasting pan on top of stove. Remove some of the excess fat. (Don't be concerned about how much fat to remove because you need some fat to absorb the flour.)
3. Over medium heat, add about 1/2 cup flour and whisk until completely blended with pan juices. Be sure to cook the juices and flour for several minutes before adding liquid. (Plan on 1/2 cup flour to about 8 cups liquid. If you need more liquid than 8 cups, leave more fat and add more flour.)
4. While stirring constantly, slowly add liquid (turkey stock, giblet stock, milk, mild vegetable juices, water, or any combination including wine or brandy) until you reach the desired consistency and amount of gravy.
5. Add cooked, chopped giblets and season to taste if needed.

Giblet Stock

1. Place the giblets and the neck in large sauce pan. Cover with water.
2. Add sliced onion, salt and pepper, celery stalks (and tops) and parsley.
3. Simmer several hours (while turkey is cooking) until gizzard is tender.
4. Pour through cheesecloth or colander, reserving liquid for the gravy.
5. Chop meat to add to the gravy.

Green Vegetables

Something green is very important in this holiday menu, not only for its visual effect, but also because everything else is very rich and it's nice to serve something fresh and simply prepared.

Green Beans

Lightly steam or simmer green beans until just barely tender; toss with sauteed slivered almonds and butter.

Broccoli

Boil in salted boiling water for 8 minutes, drain, and serve with butter.

Green Peas

Cook according to package directions and serve with water chestnuts, tiny onions, or sauteed almonds (sauté in butter and drain on paper towel).

Zucchini

This is especially good because it is still fresh at Thanksgiving. There are many ways to serve it, but we recommend lightly sauteed in butter and sprinkled with Parmesan cheese before serving.

Brussels Sprouts

1. Cut off wilted outer leaves.
2. Soak sprouts in cold, salted water for 10 minutes. Drain.
3. Cut cross-wise gashes into stem ends.
4. Place in vegetable steamer; steam until barely tender (about 10 minutes).
5. Drain and serve with one of the following:
   melted butter
   Parmesan cheese and chopped parsley
   lemon juice

Zaza's Spinach Soufflé

Serves 6

**2 packages (10-ounce each) frozen
    chopped spinach, cooked and
    squeezed dry**
1 pint sour cream
1 envelope onion soup mix
**1 full cup herb-seasoned dressing
    crumbs**
2 tablespoons melted butter

1. Cook and drain spinach. (Press water out of the spinach to make sure it's drained well and very dry.)

2. Combine the sour cream, soup mix, dressing crumbs, and melted butter. Add to spinach.

3. Place spinach mixture in buttered casserole, sprinkle more crumbs on top. Dot with butter.

4. Bake 350 degrees for 30 to 45 minutes.

Be still, my heart.

Spinach Deluxe

Serves 6

3 tablespoons butter
3 tablespoons flour
1 cup milk
1/2 pound Jack cheese, shredded
1 tablespoon grated onion
**1 package (10-ounce) frozen
    chopped spinach, cooked and
    squeezed dry**
1½ cups bread crumbs
3 eggs, beaten
salt and pepper to taste
additional bread crumbs
Parmesan cheese
melted butter

1. Melt butter in sauce pan. Add flour and stir until blended. Add milk slowly and stir until smooth and thickened.

2. Stir in cheese until melted. Remove from heat. Stir in onion and spinach. Add bread crumbs, eggs, salt and pepper to taste. Place mixture in buttered casserole.

3. Sprinkle with additional bread crumbs and Parmesan cheese. Drizzle with melted butter and bake 350 degrees 30 minutes.

Green Beans with Zucchini

Serves 6

**1 pound green beans, cleaned and
    sliced into bite-size pieces
2 medium zucchini, sliced 1/4-inch thick
4 slices bacon
1/4 cup butter
1 onion, chopped
3/4 teaspoon salt
pepper to taste**

1. Fry bacon, drain and crumble.

2. Pour bacon fat from the skillet.

3. Add butter to the skillet and sauté onion until tender.

4. Add zucchini and beans and stir-fry about 2 to 3 minutes.

5. Cover and simmer on low heat until vegetables are tender-crisp.

6. Add bacon and salt and pepper to taste.

Mushrooms and Artichokes

Serves 6

**4 tablespoons butter
3 cups fresh mushrooms, halved
1/2 cup chopped green onions
    (tops included)
2 tablespoons flour
3/4 cup turkey stock
1/4 cup milk
1 teaspoon lemon juice
1/8 teaspoon nutmeg
1 package (10-ounce) frozen
    artichoke hearts, cooked
    and drained
3/4 cup soft bread crumbs
    (1 slice bread)
1 tablespoon melted butter**

1. Heat butter and sauté mushrooms and onions. Remove with slotted spoon and set aside.

2. Blend flour in pan drippings and season with salt and pepper.

3. Add stock, milk, lemon juice and nutmeg.

4. Cook and stir until bubbly. Add all vegetables and place in 1 quart casserole.

5. Combine crumbs and butter; sprinkle around edges of casserole.

6. Bake 350 degrees for 20 to 30 minutes.

Sweet Potatoes

Stuffed Sweet Potatoes

Serves 8

4 medium oranges
8 large sweet potatoes, cooked
   and peeled
1/3 cup orange juice
2 tablespoons butter
salt and pepper to taste

1. Cut oranges in half and carefully squeeze out juice.
2. Place potatoes, orange juice, butter, salt and pepper in food processor and blend until potatoes are fluffy.
3. Scoop out the remaining pulp from the orange halves.
4. Mound potatoes into orange cups and bake 350 degrees for 20 to 25 minutes.

These make a gorgeous garnish for a big, roasted turkey and can be prepared the day ahead of time if refrigerated.

Marmalade Sweet Potatoes

Scrub the potato skins and bake 350 degrees until done (about 45 minutes). Cut cross in top of each potato. Insert a pat of butter and 1 tablespoon orange marmalade into each potato.

Sweet Potato Casserole

Serves 8

6 large sweet potatoes
1/2 cup butter
3/4 cup brown sugar
marshmallows (optional)

1. Steam sweet potatoes until tender. Remove skins.
2. Slice into bite-size pieces 1/2-inch thick.
3. Layer in casserole dish with butter and brown sugar (do this the day before).
4. Top with marshmallows and bake 350 degrees for 30 minutes. (Put this into the oven the minute you take the turkey out. By the time everything else is ready, the sweet potatoes will be too.)

Mashed Sweet Potatoes

Cook, peel, and mash potatoes. While mashing, fold in 2 tablespoons butter, orange juice and grated orange peel (or hot milk or cream, or sherry) and 2 tablespoons brown sugar until you reach the desired consistency.

Connie's Sweet Potatoes

2 cans (16-ounce each) sweet potatoes, drained
salt to taste
1 cup brown sugar
2 tablespoons cornstarch
1/2 teaspoon salt
1 cup orange juice
1/2 cup raisins
1/2 cup butter
6 tablespoons brandy, sherry, or rum
1/4 cup chopped nuts
1 teaspoon orange peel

1. Place potatoes in baking dish and sprinkle with salt to taste.
2. In a sauce pan, combine brown sugar, cornstarch and salt. Blend in orange juice and raisins.
3. Place over heat and bring to a boil, stirring constantly.
4. Add the butter, brandy, nuts and orange peel.
5. Bring to a boil. Pour over potatoes (sauce will thicken while baking).
6. Bake 45 minutes to 1 hour at 350 degrees.

Be still my heart!

Basic Cranberry Sauce

Makes 2 quarts

**1 pound cranberries (4 cups),
 washed and picked over**
2 cups water
2 cups sugar

1. Put water and sugar in large sauce pan and heat and stir until the sugar is dissolved. Boil for 5 minutes.

2. Add the cranberries. Cook, uncovered, very gently until the skins pop (about 5 minutes).

3. Chill and serve.

After the cranberries are cooked, you can add any or all of the following:

    2 teaspoons grated orange rind
    1/2 cup slivered almonds
    1 cup finely chopped apple (peeled)

Cranberry Fruit Salad Mold

Serves 8

**1 package (6-ounce) raspberry-flavored
 gelatin**
1 cup boiling water
1½ cups cold water
1 can (16-ounce) whole cranberry sauce
**1 can (11-ounce) mandarin oranges,
 drained**
2 green apples, unpeeled and diced
3/4 cup sliced celery
1/2 cup chopped walnuts

1. Dissolve gelatin in boiling water. Stir in cold water (may combine with mandarin orange juice and chill until syrupy (about 20 minutes).

2. Mix together cranberry sauce, oranges, apples, celery, and nuts.

3. Stir fruit into gelatin. Spoon into greased ring mold. Cover and chill until firm (about 4 hours).

Cranberry Chutney

Makes 2 quarts

**1 pound cranberries (4 cups),
washed and picked**
2½ cups sugar
1 cup water
6 whole cloves
2 cinnamon sticks
1/2 teaspoon salt
1 cup raisins
2 tart apples, peeled, cored and diced
2 firm pears, peeled, cored and diced
1 small onion, chopped
1/2 cup diced celery
1/2 cup coarsely chopped walnuts
1 teaspoon grated lemon peel

1. Combine cranberries, sugar, water, cloves, cinnamon, and salt and bring to a boil. Simmer until the berries pop (about 5 to 10 minutes).

2. Add raisins, apples, pears, onion, and celery. Cook, stirring constantly, until thick (about 15 minutes).

3. Remove from heat; stir in walnuts and lemon peel.

4. Spoon into sterilized jars.

This is a great hostess gift at Christmas time. It keeps at least a month. You can preserve it longer by processing jars in a water bath for 10 minutes.

Cranberry Relish

**1 pound cranberries (4 cups), washed
and picked over**
2 thin-skinned seedless oranges
2 cups sugar

1. Grind cranberries and oranges (skin included) together.

2. Stir in the sugar.

3. Place in covered jars and into the refrigerator.

4. Relish should "ripen" for a day or two before serving.

Variations

1. Grind along with the cranberries and oranges, 2 tart apples which have been quartered and cored, and 1/3 lemon (peel included).

2. Add along with the sugar, 1 cup crushed and drained pineapple and 1 teaspoon lemon juice.

3. Add along with the sugar, 1/2 to 1 cup coarsely chopped walnuts and 1 cup finely chopped celery.

Fruit Salad

Serves 8

1 large can (30-ounce) fruit cocktail
1 can (17-ounce) apricots
1/2 cup chopped dates
1 orange, peeled and sliced
1 apple, diced (do not peel)
1 large banana, sliced
1 cup whipped cream

1. Drain fruit cocktail and apricots.
2. Add dates, orange and apple.
3. Just before serving, add sliced banana.
4. Combine all with whipped cream.

You can use your imagination with this salad and combine any kind of favorite fruit in any desired amounts. Kiwi is a lovely garnish.

Experiment!

Judy's 24-Hour Fruit Salad

Serves 8

3 egg yolks
2 tablespoons sugar
2 tablespoons vinegar
1 tablespoon butter
2 tablespoons pineapple syrup (reserved)
dash salt
1 can (20½-ounce) pineapple tidbits, drained (reserve liquid)
1 large can (30-ounce) fruit cocktail, drained
2 oranges, peeled and chunked
2 cups miniature marshmallows
1 cup whipped cream

1. Combine egg yolks, sugar, vinegar, butter, pineapple syrup and salt.
2. Cook over hot water, stirring constantly until mixture coats spoon.
3. Cool to room temperature.
4. Combine fruit with marshmallows.
5. Stir egg mixture gently into fruit.
6. Fold in whipped cream.
7. Chill 24 hours before serving.

180

Hot Fruit Salad

Serves 8

1 can (29-ounce) peaches, drained
(reserve syrup)
1 can (17-ounce) apricots, drained
2 bananas, sliced
3 oranges, peeled and divided
into segments
juice of 1 lemon
peach syrup (reserved)
1 orange peel, grated
1/4 cup curacao
1 cup whipped cream (optional)

1. Place drained fruit in shallow baking dish.

2. Mix together the lemon juice and peach syrup. Pour over fruit.

3. Add grated orange peel.

4. Bake in 350 degree oven for 25 minutes. Cool slightly.

5. Pour curacao over fruit.

6. Serve warm with or without whipped cream.

Curried Fruit Bake

Serves 12

1/3 cup melted butter
3/4 cup brown sugar
1 teaspoon curry powder
1 can (17-ounce) pears, drained
1 can (29-ounce) peaches, drained
1 can (17-ounce) apricots, drained
1 can (20-ounce) pineapple chunks or
slices, drained
1 can (17-ounce) bing cherries, drained

1. Combine melted butter, brown sugar and curry powder in bottom of large baking dish.

2. Arrange fruit over butter mixture.

3. Bake 325 degrees for 30 minutes.

Classic Pumpkin Pie

Crust

This is enough dough for two 9-inch pie crusts.

> 1 cup cold shortening and butter combination (3/4 cup shortening and 1/4 cup butter)
> 2 cups flour
> 1 teaspoon salt
> 5 tablespoons ice water

1. Cut shortening, flour and salt with pastry blender until mixture resembles corn meal.

2. Add ice water.

3. Blend in lightly until dough holds together so it can be gathered into a ball.

4. Chill at least one hour before rolling.

Pumpkin Filling

This is enough filling for two 9-inch pies.

> 4 eggs, slightly beaten
> 1 can (29-ounce) pumpkin (3 cups cooked pumpkin)
> 1 cup brown sugar
> 1/2 cup white sugar
> 1 teaspoon salt
> 2 teaspoons ground cinnamon
>
> 1 teaspoon   ground ginger
> 1/2 teaspoon ground cloves
> 2 cans (13-ounce each) evaporate
>   milk ($3\frac{1}{4}$ cups half and half)
> 1 teaspoon vanilla (or 2 tablespoo
>   brandy or rum)

1. Combine all ingredients and blend well. Pour into uncooked pie shells.

2. Bake in hot oven 425 degrees for 15 minutes, reduce heat to 350 degrees and bake an additional 45 minutes. The pie is done when knife inserted in filling comes out clean.

3. Serve warm or cold with whipped cream.

If you have any apple butter, add about 1 cup to this recipe. It will add a creaminess to the pie.

You might try flavoring the whipped cream with about 2 tablespoons bourbon or sherry.

Lois' No-Bake Pumpkin Pie

Serves 8

Crust: **1¼ cups gingersnap cookie crumbs**
1/4 cup walnuts, finely chopped
1/3 cup melted butter

Combine ingredients and press firmly on bottom and sides of 9-inch pie dish. Chill.

Filling: **1 envelope unflavored gelatin**
1 teaspoon cinnamon
1/2 teaspoon ginger
1/2 teaspoon nutmeg
1/2 teaspoon salt
1 can (14-ounce) sweetened condensed milk
2 eggs, well beaten
1 can (16-ounce) pumpkin
whipped cream

1. In sauce pan, combine gelatin and spices. Stir in condensed milk and eggs. Mix well. Let stand 1 minute.

2. Over low heat, cook and stir constantly until gelatin dissolves and mixture thickens slightly (about 10 minutes).

3. Remove from heat and stir in pumpkin. Pour into crust and chill 3 or more hours. Top with whipped cream.

Frozen Pumpkin Pie

Serves 10

10-inch pie plate
1/2- to 3/4-gallon softened vanilla ice cream
2 cups pumpkin
2 teaspoons cinnamon
1/2 teaspoon ginger
1/2 teaspoon nutmeg
dash of ground cloves
2 cups whipped cream

1. Make crust of ice cream in pie plate. Freeze.

2. Cook remaining ingredients, except cream, over low heat for three minutes. Cool.

3. Fold in whipped cream and mound filling into crust. Freeze.

Peggy's Pumpkin Roll

Serves 10

3 eggs
1 cup sugar
2/3 cup pumpkin
1 teaspoon lemon juice
3/4 cup flour
1 teaspoon baking powder
2 teaspoons cinnamon
1 teaspoon ginger
1/2 teaspoon salt
1/2 teaspoon nutmeg
1 cup chopped walnuts
1 cup powdered sugar
12 ounces cream cheese, softened
4 tablespoons butter, softened
1 teaspoon vanilla
extra powdered sugar

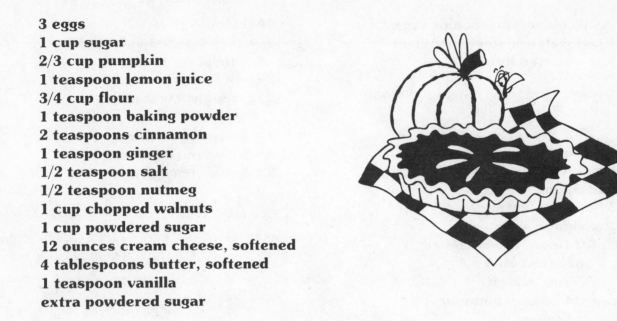

1. Beat eggs at high speed for 5 minutes. Gradually add sugar, pumpkin, and lemon juice.

2. Stir flour, baking powder, cinnamon, ginger, salt and nutmeg together and add to egg mixture.

3. Grease a jelly roll pan very well and spread mixture into pan.

4. Sprinkle mixture with chopped walnuts. Bake 375 degrees for 15 minutes.

5. Turn out immediately onto a kitchen towel which has been well dusted with powdered sugar.

6. Roll up (along with the towel) and allow to cool.

7. When cool, unroll and spread with mixture of powdered sugar, cream cheese, butter and vanilla.

8. Remove towel, roll back up and chill.

9. Dust again with powdered sugar before serving.

THE END

INDEX

INDEX, continued

INDEX, continued

NOTES

NOTES

ORDER FORM

Please send me _____ copies of **Turkey, The Bird For All Seasons** at $10.50 per copy, including postage and handling.

Enclosed is my check for $_____ payable to:

Good Time Press
15707 N.E. 153rd
Woodinville, Washington 98072

NAME _____

ADDRESS _____

CITY _____ STATE _____ ZIP _____

- -

ORDER FORM

Please send me _____ copies of **Turkey, The Bird For All Seasons** at $10.50 per copy, including postage and handling.

Enclosed is my check for $_____ payable to:

Good Time Press
15707 N.E. 153rd
Woodinville, Washington 98072

NAME _____

ADDRESS _____

CITY _____ STATE _____ ZIP _____